Utah Commission United States.

The Edmunds Act

Utah Commission United States.

The Edmunds Act

ISBN/EAN: 9783744693974

Printed in Europe, USA, Canada, Australia, Japan

Cover: Foto ©ninafisch / pixelio.de

More available books at **www.hansebooks.com**

UTAH COMMISSION.

The Edmunds Act,

REPORTS OF THE COMMISSION,

RULES, REGULATIONS AND DECISIONS,

AND

POPULATION, REGISTRATION AND ELECTION TABLES, &C.

FOR THE INFORMATION OF REGISTRATION AND ELECTION OFFICERS IN UTAH.

SALT LAKE CITY, UTAH:
TRIBUNE PRINTING AND PUBLISHING COMPANY.
1883.

TABLE OF CONTENTS.

	PAGE.
Act of Congress, "The Edmunds,"	3
Election August 6, 1883, Offices to be Filled	36
Letter to the Secretary of the Interior Nov. 17, 1882, Reporting Progress	9
Letter to the Secretary of the Interior August 24, 1883	109
Oath for Voters under Laws of Utah	28
Oath for Voters under Rules of the Utah Commission	29
Order, September 1, 1882, for the Guidance of Registration Officers	30
Order, September 6, 1882, Instructions to Registration Officers	31
Order, September 11, 1882, Relating to Selection of Judges of Election	32
Order, October 19, 1882, Eligibility of Female non-Taxpayers to Vote	32
Order, October 28, 1882, Instructions to Judges of Election	33
Order, Nov. 3, 1882, Appointing Board of Canvasers for Delegate Election	34
Order, June 13, 1883, Relating to Eligibility of Wm. Jennings to register and vote	35
Order, June 18, 1883, Instructing Election Judges	38
Order, July 2, 1883, Offices to be filled at approaching election	39
Order, Aug. 14, 1883, Appointing Board of Canvassers	40
Order, Aug. 24, 1883, Relating to disqualified persons who may be elected to office	41
Order, Appointing T. C. Bailey, Registrar Salt Lake City, adopted Jan. 17, 1884	119
Order, To Govern Registration Officers, adopted Jan. 22, 1884	119
Report of the Utah Commission Aug. 31, 1882	6
Resolutions, Aug. 21, 1882, Relating to Election of Delegate to Congress	14
Rules to Govern Registration Officers, election 1882	15
Rules to Govern Judges of Election, election 1882	19
Rules for the Guidance of Registration Officers, election 1883	22
Rules to Govern Judges of Election, 1883	25
Report of the Utah Commission October 30, 1883	110
Supplemental Rules to Govern Registration Officers, adopted Jan. 23, 1884	120
Supplemental Instructions for Registration Officers, Jan. 23, 1884	121

TABLES.

Population of Utah by Counties and Nativity in 1880	43
Population, Native and Foreign Born	45
Population of Utah by Race and by Counties	46
Population of Utah by School, Military, Citizenship, Ages, &c	47
Population of Utah by Age, Native and Foreign Born	48
Population of Utah, Native and Foreign Born, all Ages	50
Population of Minor Civil Division	51
Table, Registration of 1882	54
Table, Registration and Election Returns for Election of Nov. 7, 1882	57
Table, Analytical of the Registration and Election for Delegate to Congress 1882	64
Table, Abstract "A," Registration 1883	65
Table, Official Returns Election Aug. 6, 1883	71

THE "EDMUNDS ACT."

AN ACT to amend section fifty-three hundred and fifty-two of the Revised Statutes of the United States, in reference to bigamy, and for other purposes.

Be it enacted by the Senate and House of Representatives of the United States of America in Congress assembled, That section fifty-three hundred and fifty-two of the Revised Statutes of the United States be, and the same is hereby, amended so as to read as follows, namely:

"Every person who has a husband or wife living who, in a Territory or other place over which the United States have exclusive jurisdiction, hereafter marries another, whether married or single, and any man who hereafter simultaneously, or on the same day, marries more than one woman, in a Territory or other place over which the United States have exclusive jurisdiction, is guilty of polygamy, and shall be punished by a fine of not more than five hundred dollars and by imprisonment for a term of not more than five years; but this section shall not extend to any person by reason of any former marriage whose husband or wife by such marriage shall have been absent for five successive years, and is not known to such person to be living, and is believed by such person to be dead, nor to any person by reason of any former marriage which shall have been dissolved by a valid decree of a competent court, nor to any person by reason of any former marriage which shall have been pronounced void by a valid decree of a competent court, on the ground of nullity of the marriage contract."

SEC. 2. That the foregoing provisions shall not affect the prosecution or punishment of any offense already committed against the section amended by the first section of this act.

SEC. 3. That if any male person, in a Territory or other place over which the United States have exclusive jurisdiction, hereafter cohabits with more than one woman, he shall be deemed guilty of a misdemeanor, and on conviction thereof shall be punished by a fine of not more than three hundred dollars, or by imprisonment for not more than six months, or by both said punishments, in the discretion of the court,

SEC. 4. That counts for any or all of the offenses named in sections one and three of this act may be joined in the same information or indictment.

SEC. 5. That in any prosecution for bigamy, polygamy, or unlawful cohabitation, under any statute of the United States, it shall be sufficient cause of challenge to any person drawn or summoned as a juryman or talesman, first, that he is or has been living in the practice of bigamy, polygamy, or unlawful cohabitation with more than one woman, or that he is or has been guilty of an offense punishable by either of the foregoing sections, or by section fifty-three hundred and fifty-two of the Revised Statutes of the United States, or the act of July first, eighteen hundred and sixty-two, entitled "An act to punish and prevent the practice of polygamy in the Territories of the United States and other places, and disapproving and annulling certain acts of the legislative assembly of the Territory of Utah," or, second, that he believes it right for a man to have more than one living and undivorced wife at the same time, or to live in the practice of cohabiting with more than one woman; and any person appearing or offered as a juror or talesman, and challenged on either of the foregoing grounds, may be questioned on his oath as to the existence of any such cause of challenge, and other evidence may be introduced bearing upon the question raised by such challenge; and this question shall be tried by the court But as to the first ground of challenge before mentioned, the person challenged shall not be bound to answer if he shall say upon his oath that he declines on the ground that his answer may tend to criminate himself; and if he shall answer as to said first ground, his answer shall not be given in evidence in any criminal prosecution against him for any offense named in sections one or three of this act; but if he declines to answer on any ground, he shall be rejected as incompetent.

SEC. 6. That the President is hereby authorized to grant amnesty to such classes of offenders guilty of bigamy, polygamy, or unlawful cohabitation, before the passage of this act, on such conditions and under such limitations as he shall think proper; but no such amnesty shall have effect unless the conditions thereof shall be complied with.

SEC. 7. That the issue of bigamous or polygamous marriages, known as Mormon marriages, in cases in which such marriages have been solemnized according to the ceremonies of the Mormon sect, in any Territory of the United States, and such issue shall have been born before the first day of January, anno Domini eighteen hundred and eighty-three, are hereby legitimated.

SEC 8. That no polygamist, bigamist, or any person cohabiting with more than one woman, and no woman cohabiting with any of the persons described as aforesaid in this section, in any Territory or other place over which the United States have exclusive jurisdiction, shall be entitled to vote at any election held in any such Territory or other place, or be eligible for election or appointment to or be entitled to hold any office or place of public trust, honor, or emolument in, under, or for any such Territory or place, or under the United States.

SEC. 9. That all the registration and election offices of every description in the Territory of Utah are hereby declared vacant, and each and every duty relating to the registration of voters, the conduct of elections, the receiving or rejection of votes, and the canvassing and returning of the same, and the issuing of certificates or other evidence of election in said Territory, shall, until other provisions be made by the legislative assembly of said Territory as is hereinafter by this section provided, be performed under the existing laws of the United States and said Territory by proper persons, who shall be appointed to execute such offices and perform such duties by a board of five persons, to be appointed by the President, by and with the advice and consent of the Senate, not more than three of whom shall be members of one political party; and a majority of whom shall be a quorum. The members of said board so appointed by the President shall each receive a salary at the rate of three thousand dollars per annum, and shall continue in office until the legislative assembly of said Territory shall make provision for filling said offices as herein authorized. The secretary of the Territory shall be the secretary of said board, and keep a journal of its proceedings, and attest the action of said board under this section. The canvass and return of all the votes at elections in said Territory for members of the legislative assembly thereof shall also be returned to said board, which shall canvass all such returns and issue certificates of election for those persons who, being eligible for such election, shall appear to have been lawfully elected, which certificates shall be the only evidence of the right of such persons to sit in such assembly; *Provided*, That said board of five persons shall not exclude any person otherwise eligible to vote from the polls on account of any opinion such person may entertain on the subject of bigamy or polygamy, nor shall they refuse to count any such vote on account of the opinion of the person casting it on the subject of bigamy or polygamy; but each house of such assembly, after its organization, shall have power to decide upon the elections and qualifications of its members. And at, or after the first meeting of said legislative assembly whose members shall have been elected and returned according to the provisions of this act, said legislative assembly may make such laws, conformable to the organic act of said Territory and not inconsistent with other laws of the United States, as it shall deem proper concerning the filling of the offices in said Territory declared vacant by this act.

Approved, March 22, 1882.

REPORT

OF

THE UTAH COMMISSION.

OFFICE OF THE UTAH COMMISSION,
Salt Lake City, Utah, August 31, 1882.

DEAR SIR: The Commission appointed by the President, under the ninth section of "An act to amend section 5352 of the Revised Statutes of the United States, in reference to bigamy, and for other purposes," approved March 22, 1882, respectfully report: That all the members of the Commission met, by request of the chairman, at the city of Chicago, on the 17th of July, 1882, and remained in session several days. James R. Pettigrew, of Arkansas, a member of the Commission, was appointed temporary Secretary. After consultation and an examination and consideration of the laws of the United States and of the Territory of Utah pertaining to our duties, it was determined that nothing could be done in regard to the registration of voters and the conduct of any election in Utah until the necessary appropriation bills then pending in Congress should be passed. Accordingly, the Commission adjourned to meet at Omaha, Neb., on the 15th day of August, where the Commissioners met, and on the following day commenced their journey to this city, arriving here on the evening of the 18th instant.

On the day following a session was held for the transaction of business, Arthur L. Thomas, Secretary of the Territory, and ex-officio Secretary of the Commission, being present, and one or more sessions have been held each day since. A strong disposition with some of the non-Mormon citizens against preparing for the election of a Delegate in Congress manifested itself before the work of preparation therefor was commenced. But upon investigation as to the condition of affairs, and an examination as to the state of the law and the duty of the Commission thereunder, the following preamble and resolution was adopted:

Whereas it is provided by the Revised Statutes of the United States (section 1862) that every Territory shall have the right to send a Delegate to the House of Representatives of the United States, and as it is further provided (section 25) that such election shall be held in all the Territories of the United States on the Tuesday after the first Monday in November, 1882: Therefore,

Resolved, That in order to prepare for such election in the Territory of Utah on the day so established the Commission will proceed forthwith to appoint registration officers to revise the registration lists, now on file in the office of the clerks of each of the several counties, in the manner required by law.

In pursuance of this resolution the Commission proceeded with great care and deliberation to prepare "rules and regulations" for the guidance of the registration and election officers to be appointed. This was a difficult and delicate task, because of the necessity of framing the rules and regulations governing the registration of voters and the conduct of the election to conform to the principles and requirements of the act of Congress as well as the laws of the Territory. We inclose a printed copy of the same, together with the forms of affidavits, etc., provided by the Commission.

The matter of the appointment of registration officers for the several counties in the Territories was then taken up, and one for each county has been duly appointed and commissioned. In addition to these a deputy or assistant in each voting precinct in the Territory will be immediately appointed. Our selections have and must necessarily be influenced in a considerable degree by suggestions and recommendations of leading citizens here. The embarrassments in this direction have been great, but the Commission have endeavored to secure the very best available men, rejecting, of course, all persons who are ineligible under the law.

From present indications it appears that that class of persons who are deprived of the right of suffrage by the act of Congress will not attempt to register or vote. These will number, male and female, probably 10,000 voters. Many of the non-Mormons have hitherto refrained from voting, but it is believed that at the November election they will cast a much larger vote than at any time heretofore. However, the business of the Commission, as understood by the members thereof, relates not to the questions of parties nor candidates, but to securing so far as possible a fair registration and an impartially conducted election under the law.

As before suggested, the Commission have encountered many embarrassments and complications. The opposition made at the outset by some non-Mormons of respectability and influence against holding the regular election for Delegate in Congress, as required by law, in November next, was an unpleasant feature of the situation. But there does not appear to be under the law any discretion whatever for the Commission. The law demanded an election. The people of the Territory were clearly entitled to representation in Congress, if the same could be secured through a due observance of the restrictions imposed in relation to bigamy and polygamy. We did not see how we could excuse the omission, if being present and prepared to proceed with the work assigned us we should not even attempt to perform this manifest duty, and so it was decided to proceed. It was not deemed advisable, even if the power was in the Commission, concerning which there is some doubt, to commence *de novo* a registration of the voters of the Territory; but after very careful consideration it was decided to order a revision of the existing registration lists in September, as required by the Territorial law, applying to the same the governing principles of the Edmunds act.

We think the regularity of this proceeding cannot be questioned. Its effectiveness will be equal to an entirely new registration, and we believe the results of the election will so demonstrate. In the preparation of the rules and regulations to govern the registration and the conduct of the election, as before stated, the labor of assimilating the acts of Congress and the local election law, was tedious and perplexing, involving much greater responsibility than was agreeable to the Commission to assume; but to accomplish the results required by the provisions of section 8 of the Edmunds act it became necessary to use all the powers conferred.

A later embarrassment came in the form of a demand on the part of certain non-Mormon citizens of high character that the Commission should assume jurisdiction and decide the local statute authorizing women to vote to be illegal and void. We concluded that it was not competent for the Commission to repeal or modify that statute in the manner suggested; that the principle of female suffrage is, in no respect, in conflict with the purposes of the Edmunds law, and, therefore, that the Commission had nothing whatever to do with the subject; moreover, we found on investigation that this statute had been in force for twelve years without being adjudicated in the Courts of the Territory or disturbed by Congress. In conclusion, permit us to say that we believe the results to be reached through the careful registration already insured, and the impartial election which can hardly fail to follow, will be satisfactory to the government and the country.

In closing this report, it is due to the Territorial Secretary, who is ex-officio Secretary of the Commission, Mr. Arthur L. Thomas, to say that the Commission has received from him valuable assistance in its work, particularly in the matter of the selection of registration and other officers.

Very respectfully, your obedient servants,

ALEX. RAMSEY,
A. S. PADDOCK,
G. L. GODFREY,
A. B. CARLTON,
J. R. PETTIGREW,
Commissioners.

Hon. H. M. TELLER,
Secretary of the Interior, Washington, D. C.

OFFICE OF THE UTAH COMMISSION,
Salt Lake City, Utah, November 17, 1882.

SIR: The election for Delegate to Congress having been held in Utah Territory on the 7th inst., under the supervision of this Commission, we deem it proper to report to your department the progress made up to this time in the discharge of our trust.

Since our last report, dated August 31, we appointed a registration officer for each voting precinct of the several counties, and established some additional polling places, with a view of affording proper facilities for all the legal voters. In order to conform the local law, so far as practicable, to the requirements of the act of Congress, we were obliged to promulgate rules and regulations for the judges of election.

We next appointed judges of election, three for each polling place, about seven hundred and fifty in number. The local law requires that the judges shall be selected from both political parties, if practicable. Accordingly we selected them, in general, from both parties; but in some instances we were obliged to appoint all of them from the "Liberal party" or from the "People's party," because there were no eligible and qualified persons, so far as we were informed, in such precincts belonging to the other party. Commissions were sent to each of the judges (copies of which, together with the rules and regulations, are herewith inclosed).

In order to procure such information as we deemed useful to the government, we addressed circulars to the registrars, and from their responses we learn that the total number of registered voters is 33,266, of whom 18,772 are males, and 14,494 are females. From their reports it appears that about 12,000 men and women are excluded from registration by reason of polygamy.

Several of the counties of this Territory are quite large in area, some of them over a hundred miles long, sparsely inhabited, and difficult of access by mail or otherwise. This has occasioned considerable delay and extra exertion in preparing for the election and receiving the returns.

The anomalous condition of this country and its people, together with the inherent difficulty of adjusting the local laws to the act of Congress, are such that they imposed on us great care and deliberation, lest, on the one hand, we should go beyond the limits of the law, or, on the other hand, fall short of a vigorous and effective discharge of our duties.

In the absence of instructions or judicial decisions to aid us in the interpretation of the law prescribing our duties, we were obliged to construe it for ourselves, and in doing so we endeavored to conform to the well-known canons for the construction of statutes, having a due regard for the evident intention of Congress in this act, construed with other acts of Congress, *in pari materia.*

"Polygamists and bigamists," and persons "cohabiting with more than one woman," are, by section 8, to be excluded from voting and holding office.

Immediately upon addressing ourselves to the discharge of our duties, we were obliged to consider the scope and extent of this exclusion.

Did Congress intend that those only should be excluded, who, *at the very time* of the registration or election, were *then* living in polygamy, or in "unlawful cohabitation with more than one woman?" If so, such a construction would render this section a perfect nullity. The means of evasion are patent to the dullest comprehension. We therefore concluded that neither the letter nor spirit of the statute required such a narrow construction, and, in our published "Rules and Regulations," we gave the exclusion a wider scope and application.

We found that the local law prescribed a certain form of oath to be taken by persons applying to be registered as voters. We adopted this oath *verbatim*, adding a clause in regard to "polygamy and bigamy," and "unlawful cohabitation," which we considered it proper to do, in order to make the local law conform, so far as practicable, to the principles and requirements of the act of Congress.

In short, we were charged by the act of Congress with the duty of excluding from the polls and from eligibility to office, a certain class of persons. How this was to be done was not defined by the act.

Were we to exclude only those who had been convicted of the crime of polygamy in the Courts? This construction would have been derided by everybody in this Territory.

We concluded that it was the intention of Congress to leave it largely to the discretion of the Commission, to determine the means of discriminating between the legal and illegal voters. This we endeavored to do in part by the prescribed oath, which sets forth the various qualifications of a legal voter, *e. g.*, those in regard to age, residence, citizenship or naturalization, and freedom from the disqualifications imposed by act of Congress.

During the week before the November election the Commission made an order appointing five gentlemen of character and standing as a Board of Canvassers of the returns of the election for a Delegate to the Forty-eighth Congress (a copy of which order is enclosed herein). On the 16th day of November, 1882, the said Board of Canvassers met at the rooms of the Commission and canvassed the election returns, from which it appeared that John T. Caine had received 23,039 votes, and Philip T. Van Zile had received 4,884 votes. John T. Caine having received a majority of all the legal votes, he was declared duly elected, and a certificate given accordingly.

Having reason to believe that it is expected by the Executive that this Commission will make suggestions as to any additional legislation that may be needed to carry out the principles of the law under which the Commission was organized, we would state that, in our judgment, a marriage law enacted by Congress would be an efficient auxiliary in the suppression of polygamy. It is asserted, and generally believed by non-Mormons in this Territory, that plural marriage is still practiced here in secret. We would recommend that Congress enact a law declaring all future marriages in this Territory null and void, unless they are contracted and evidenced in the manner provided by the act. For example: That all marriages shall be solemnized in certain designated public places; and witnessed by such persons, and registered in such public offices, as to make the proof of marriage morally certain; providing also, that the person officiating in the marriage ceremony, together with the parties and witnesses, shall make their affidavits against polygamy, and set forth the time and place and other particulars relating to the marriage. Or, allow marriages to be solemnized in private; but with the like guarantees of registration, affidavits, witnesses, etc., and in either case providing penalties for violation of the act by any of the persons concerned therein. In making this suggestion, we omit the details, which can readily be supplied by reference to the marriage acts of most of the States.

In our former report we adverted to the law of this Territory conferring on women the right of suffrage. This law was enacted by the Territorial Legislature some twelve years ago. Of course it is competent for Congress to repeal or annul this law. Without expressing any opinion on the question of women suffrage in general, we are satisfied that, owing to the peculiar state of affairs in Utah, this law is an obstruction to the speedy solution of the "vexed question."

In the prosecution of polygamy cases here it is difficult to prove the first or legal marriage. We would suggest, as a remedy, that the first or legal wife be declared by act of Congress a competent witness in such prosecutions.

Under the act of Congress, by virtue of whose provisions this Commission was appointed, the people of Utah appear to be put upon probation until a legislative assembly, elected under the provisions of the act, shall meet and pass the requisite laws concerning registration and election.

The election for members of the legislative assembly will be held next August, and that body will hold its next session in January, 1884. It is to be hoped that it will comprise a sufficient number of members who will be disposed to bring this Territory into harmony with the sentiments of the people of other parts of the country.

We have been engaged in the discharge of our trust, only a few months, not long enough to fully test the operation of the law as to its ultimate results. But, so far, it has been a decided success in excluding polygamists from the exercise of suffrage; and we are of the opinion that the steady and continued enforcement of the law will place polygamy in a condition of gradual extinction, and that the domination that is complained of by non-Mormons in Utah and elsewhere, will, at no distant day, be much ameliorated.

In accepting the trust committed to us, it was not expected by the Commission, and, we suppose, not anticipated by Congress nor the Executive Department of the Government, that the desired results would be accomplished at once nor in the brief space of a few months; but there is reason to believe that the operation of this law and other influences are setting strongly in the direction of reform, and that the hitherto dominant faction will be supplanted by "Young Utah" in the conduct of public affairs.

There is no doubt that the enactment of the law of Congress under which this Commission was appointed has agitated the public mind in this Territory to a remarkable degree. Hitherto there has been very little public discussion of political questions, and in general the people have not attended political meetings in large numbers. But we are gratified to find that in the "campaign" preceding the November election for Delegate to Congress, the people of all classes have manifested a lively interest in public affairs, and have attended the political meetings in large numbers. Many of these meetings have been held by both parties in various parts of the Territory, and able addresses have been delivered by speakers on both sides. It is an encouraging sign that many of the "Liberal" meetings have been largely attended by Mormons, and in many instances they have composed the chief part of the audiences. It is proper to add that so far as we have learned these meetings have been characterized by exceptional good order, good humor, and decorum. On Saturday night before the election both parties held large mass meetings in Salt Lake City, and vied with each other in the display of national flags and patriotic music.

Our attention has been called to the propriety of our recommending Congressional legislation of a radical character. But we are not inclined to advise such measures, unless upon further observation and experience the wisdom and necessity of such legislation shall be demonstrated.

The area of the Territory is 84,000 square miles. The population is about 150,000, about 40,000 being non-Mormons, many of whom are socalled apostates from the Mormon church.

The people are generally engaged in agricultural pursuits. Prior to the completion of the Union Pacific and Central Pacific railroads there were very few non-Mormon residents in the Territory. Since 1869 the business of mining has become an important interest, and from that time the total output is over $60,000,000 in silver, lead, and gold.

There are also valuable deposits of coal, iron, copper, and other minerals. The mines give employment to a great many persons, and have been the means of attracting a large non-Mormon population to the Territory. Many of the non-Mormons (or "Gentiles) are doing a prosperous business in banking, mining and mercantile pursuits.

The legislation of Congress, as we understand it, is not enacted against the religion of any portion of the people of this Territory. The law under which we are acting is directed against the crime of polygamy, for the extirpation of which this Commission will freely use all the powers delegated to us, and will from time to time suggest to the Government such supplemental legislation as may aid in suppressing this reproach to the civilization of this age and country.

We trust that this object will be accomplished without resorting to measures destructive to local self government, punishing the whole people, the innocent as well as the guilty, with political ostracism. At all events we are unwilling to advise such a course until the act of Congress under which we are acting shall be more fully tested. Besides, a proper respect for the legislative branch of the government would restrain us from impeaching the wisdom of their enactment at the very threshold of the work committed to us, and long before the time expressed in the act of Congress.

If, however, the next session of the legislative assembly, elected under the act of Congress, shall fail to respond to the will of the nation, Congress should have no hesitation in using extraordinary measures to compel the people of this Territory to obey the laws of the land.

For the Commission:

Very respectfully,

ALEX. RAMSEY,
Chairman.

Hon. Henry M. Teller,
Secretary of the Interior, Washington, D. C.

RESOLUTION

ADOPTED BY THE UTAH COMMISSION, MONDAY, AUGUST 21st, 1882.

WHEREAS, It is provided by the Revised Statutes of the United States, (Sec. 1862) that every Territory shall have the right to send a Delegate to the House of Representatives of the United States, and as it is further provided, (Sec. 25) that such election shall be held in all the Territories of the United States, on the Tuesday after ter the first Monday in November, 1882, therefore,

Resolved, That in order to prepare for such election in the Territory of Utah, on the day so established, the Commission will proceed forthwith to appoint registration officers to revise the registration lists now on file in the office of the clerks of each of the several counties in the manner required by law.

RULES

ADOPTED BY THE UTAH COMMISSION, DEFINING THE DUTIES OF REGISTRATION OFFICERS, FOR THE REGISTRATION COMMENCING SEPTEMBER 11, AND ENDING SEPTEMBER 16, 1882.

RULE I.

There shall be appointed one Registration Officer for each county, and one Deputy Registration Officer for each precinct thereof.

RULE II.

Such Registration officer shall, on the 2nd Monday in September next, proceed, by himself and his deputies in the manner following: The Registration Officer of each county shall procure from the office of the Clerk of the County Court, the last preceding Registry list on file in his office, and shall by himself or his deputies require of each person whose name is on said list, to take and subscribe the following oath or affirmation:

TERRITORY OF UTAH, } ss.
COUNTY OF .... }

I..............., being first duly sworn, (or affirmed) depose and say, that I am over twenty-one years of age, and have resided in the Territory of Utah for six months, and in the precinct of..... .... one month immediately preceding the date hereof, and (if a male) am a native born or naturalized (as the case may be) citizen of the United States, and a tax payer in this Territory, (or if a female), I am native born, or naturalized, or the wife, widow, or daughter, (as the case may be) of a native born or naturalized citizen of the United States; and I do further solemnly swear (or affirm) that I am not a bigamist nor a polygamist; that I have not violated the laws of the United States prohibiting bigamy or polygamy; that I do not live or cohabit with more than one woman in the marriage relation, nor does any relation exist between me and any woman which has been entered into, or continued in violation of the said laws of the United States prohibiting bigamy or polygamy; (and if a woman) that I am not the wife of a polygamist, nor have I entered into any relation with any man in violation of the laws of the United States concerning polygamy or bigamy.

Subscribed and sworn to before me this....day of......188..
....
Registration Officer .... Precinct.

And said Registration Officer, or his deputies, shall add to said lists the names of all qualified voters in such precinct whose names are not on the list, upon their taking and subscribing to the aforesaid oath, and the said Registration Officers shall strike from said lists the names of all persons who fail or refuse to take said oath, or who have died or removed from the precinct, or are disqualified as voters under the Act of Congress approved March 22d, A. D. 1882, entitled "An Act to amend Section 5352 of the Revised Statutes of the United States in reference to bigamy, and for other purposes; *Provided*, That if the Registration Officer be unable to procure the Registration lists from the office of the Clerk of the County Court of any county, or if the same have been lost or destroyed, the said officer and his deputies shall make a new Registry list in full of all legal voters of each precinct in the county under the provisions of these rules; and, *Provided*, further, That the action of any Registration Officer may be revised and reversed by this Commission upon a proper showing.

RULE III.

Upon the completion of the lists it shall be the duty of each Registration Officer to prepare triplicate lists in alphabetical order for each precinct containing the names of all registered voters, one of which lists, together with the affidavits, shall be filed in the office of the Clerk of the County Court; one list he shall cause to be posted up in each precinct at least fifteen days before the day of election, at or near the place of the election, and the other lists shall be transmitted by him to the Judges of Election of the several precincts for use at the polls.

RULE IV.

Voters removing from one election precinct to another in the same county may appear before the Registration Officer at any time previous to the filing of the lists in the office of the Clerk of the County Court, and have their names erased therefrom, and they may thereupon have their names registered in the precinct to which they may remove.

RULE V.

The Registration Officer of each county shall cause to be written or printed a notice which shall designate the office, or offices to be filled, and stating that the election will commence at.......... (designating the place for holding the polls), one hour after sunrise, and continue until sunset on the.....day of.........., A. D. 18...

Dated at...............on this....day of................,
A. D. 18...

....
Registration Officer.

A copy of which shall be posted up, at least fifteen days before the election, in the three public places in the precinct best calculated to give notice to all the voters. It shall be the duty of the Registration Officer to give notice on the lists posted as aforesaid, that the Deputy Registration Officer of each precinct will hear objections to the right to vote of any person registered, until sunset of the fifth day preceding the day of election. Said objections shall be made by a qualified voter, in writing, and delivered to said Deputy Registration Officer, who shall issue a written notice to the person objected to, stating the place, day and hour, when the objection shall be heard. The person making the objection shall serve, or cause to be served, said notice on the person objected to, and shall also make return of such service to the Deputy Registration Officer, before whom the objection is to be heard. Upon the hearing of the case, if said officer shall find that the person objected to is not a qualified voter, he shall within three days prior to the election transmit a certified list of all such disqualified persons to the Judges of Election appointed by this Commission; and said Judges shall strike such names from the Registry lists before the opening of the polls.

RULE VI.

This Commission will appoint three capable and discreet persons, who are eligible under said Act of Congress, in each precinct of the several counties to act as Judges of Election, one at least of whom shall be of the political party that was in the minority at the last previous election, if any such party there be in such precinct. And the persons who shall be appointed Registration Officers in each county are required as soon as may be, after their appointment, to transmit to the Secretary of this Commission, by mail, at Salt Lake City, the names of three persons, who are proper and eligible persons to act as Judges of Election in each precinct of the county, for the information of this Commission. The Secretary of this Commission will make out certificates of said appointments, and transmit the same by mail or other safe conveyance to the persons so appointed, who, previous to entering upon said office, shall take and subscribe an oath, or affirmation, that they will, well and faithfully, perform all the duties thereof, to the best of their ability, and that they will studiously endeavor to prevent any fraud, deceit, or abuse of any election over which they may preside, and that they are not bigamists or polygamists. If in any precinct any of such persons appointed Judges decline to serve, or fail to appear, the Deputy Registration Officer of the precinct shall appoint a Judge, or Judges, to fill the vacancy, and the persons so appointed shall qualify as herein provided.

RULE VII.

After the canvass shall have been completed, the Judges of Election shall add up and determine the number of votes cast for each person for the several offices, which result shall be placed on the lists made by the Judges acting as Clerks of the Election; and the Judges shall thereupon certify to the same, and shall forward all the lists securely sealed by mail, or other safe conveyance, to the Secretary of this Commission, at Salt Lake City, Utah, and the ballot box shall be transmitted to the office of the Clerk of the County Court.

RULE VIII.

The Registration Officers and their deputies shall hold their offices during the pleasure of this Commission, and shall each, before entering upon the discharge of his duties, take and subscribe an oath in substance that "he will support the Constitution of the United States, and will faithfully and impartially perform the duties of his office as herein defined, and that he is not a bigamist or polymist."

RULE IX.

The County Registration Officers, and their deputies, shall receive compensation as follows: For County Registration Officers, $4 per day; for Each Registration Officer, $3 per day, the compensation to be paid for the time during which said officers have been necessarily employed in the discharge of their duties, and the Judges of Election shall receive compensation as follows: $3 per day for conducting the election, and 30 cents an hour for the time necessarily employed canvassing the votes, and all of said officers are authorized to administer all oaths required in the registration and conduct of the election.

RULES

ADOPTED BY THE UTAH COMMISSION DEFINING THE DUTIES OF JUDGES OF ELECTION FOR THE ELECTION FOR DELEGATE HELD ON NOVEMBER 7, 1882.

RULE I.

The Judges will conform to Rules 6 and 7 of the Rules and Regulation heretofore adopted by this Commission, which are as follows:

RULE 6. This Commission will appoint three capable and discreet persons, who are eligible under said Act of Congress, in each precinct of the several counties to act as Judges of Election, one at least of whom shall be of the political power that was in the minority at the last previous election, if any such party there be in such precinct. And the persons who shall be appointed Registration Officers in each county are required as soon as may be, after their appointment, to transmit to the Secretary of this Commission, by mail, at Salt Lake City, the names of three persons, who are proper and eligible persons to act as Judges of Election in each precinct of the county for the information of this Commission. The Secretary of this Commission will make out certificates of said appointments, and transmit the same by mail or other safe conveyance to the persons so appointed, who, previous to entering upon said office, shall take and subscribe an oath, or affirmation, that they will, well and faithfully, perform all the duties thereof, to the best of their ability, and that they will studiously endeavor to prevent any fraud, deceit, or abuse of any election over which they may preside, and that they are not bigamists or polygamists. If in any precinct any of such persons appointed Judges decline to serve, or fail to appear, the Deputy Registration Officer of the precinct shall appoint a Judge or Judges to fill the vacancy, and the persons so appointed shall qualify as herein provided.

RULE 7. After the canvass shall have been completed the Judges of Election shall add up and determine the number of votes cast for each person for the several offices, which result shall be placed on the lists made by the Judges acting as Clerks of the Election; and the Judges shall thereupon certify to the same, and shall forward all the lists securely sealed by mail, or other safe conveyance, to the Secretary of this Commission, at Salt Lake City, Utah.

RULE II.

The Judges of Election will take the oath of office before any Notary Public, Justice of the Peace, or other officer authorized to administer oaths, and send said oath immediately by mail to the Secretary of this Commission as an evidence of acceptance of the office.

RULE III.

The Commission will provide the necessary books, blanks, stationary and envelopes for each voting precinct; and the Judges of Election will procure the ballot boxes from the Clerks of the County Courts.

RULE IV.

Before opening the polls, the ballot box shall be carefully and publicly examined by the Judges of Election, who shall satisfy themselves that nothing is therein. It shall then be locked and the key delivered to the presiding Judge; and said ballot box shall not be opened during the election.

RULE V.

At the opening of the polls on the day of election, the Judges of Election for their respective precincts shall designate one of the Judges acting as Clerk, who shall have in custody the Registry of voters, and shall make the entries therein required by law; the other of said Judges acting as Clerk shall write the name of each person voting, and opposite to it the number of the vote. Every voter shall designate on a single ballot, written or printed, the name of the person voted for, with a pertinent designation of the office to be filled, which ballot shall be neatly folded and placed in one of the envelopes herein before provided for, and delivered to the presiding Judge of Election, who shall, in the presence of the voter, on the name of the proposed voter being found on the Registry, and all challenges to such vote being decided in favor of such voter, deposit it in the ballot-box without any mark whatever being placed on such ballot or envelope; otherwise the ballot shall be rejected.

RULE VI.

Challenge shall be allowed at the polls for cause, by any qualified voter, and the Judges of the Election, or a majority of them, shall hear and immediately decide upon any challenge that may be made. If the challenge is on account of alleged want of citizenship, and it appears that the voter is a person of foreign birth, he shall not be allowed to vote except on producing his naturalization papers, or proving that such papers have been issued and lost or destroyed. And if the voter, being a person of foreign birth, claims the right to vote by reason of being the wife of a naturalized citizen, or that he, or she, has become a citizen by reason of the naturalization of his or her parents, the Judges shall receive the vote upon satisfactory oral proof, without requiring the production of the naturalization papers of the husband or parents.

RULE VII.

As soon as the polls shall be closed, the Judges of Election shall immediately proceed to canvass the votes cast at such election, and continue without adjournment until completed. And all candidates voted for may be present in person, or by representative, to witness and count. If any envelope contains two or more ballots of the same kind folded together, only one shall be counted.

RULE VIII.

The canvass shall commence by the Judges, who have acted as Clerks of the Election, comparing their respective lists, and ascertaining from said lists the number of votes cast. The box shall then be opened, and the ballots therein taken out and counted by the Judges, and the Judges, acting as Clerks, shall each make a list of all the persons voted for. The presiding Judge shall then proceed to open the ballots and call off therefrom the names of the persons voted for, and the offices they are intended to fill; and the Judges, acting as Clerks, shall take an account of the same upon their list, and all the ballots shall be returned to the ballot box, and the ballot box shall be locked and securely sealed; and the box with the ballots enclosed shall be preserved by the presiding Judge of the Election for twenty days after the day of the election; and said ballot box, with the ballots enclosed, shall be forwarded to this Commission immediately on being required to do so by the Commission. If not so required, the ballots shall be destroyed by the presiding Judge of the Election, and the ballot boxes shall be transmitted to the office of the Clerk of the County Court.

RULE IX.

The Judge of Election shall open the polls one hour after sunrise, and close at sunset.

RULE X.

The Judge of Election shall receive compensation as follows: $3 per day for conducting the election, and 30 cents an hour for the time necessarily employed canvassing the votes, and all of said officers are authorized to administer all oaths required in the registration and conduct of the election.

NOTE.—Whenever any ballot shall be deposited in the ballot box, the Judge having the Registry list shall write the word "VOTED" opposite the name of the person casting the vote.

RULES

ADOPTED BY THE UTAH COMMISSION DEFINING THE DUTIES OF REGISTRATION OFFICERS, FOR THE REGISTRATION COMMENCING JUNE 4 AND ENDING JUNE 9, 1883.

RULE I.

There shall be appointed one Registration Officer for each county, and one Deputy Registration Officer for each precinct thereof.

RULE II.

Said Registration Officer shall, on or before the first Monday in June, procure from the office of the Clerk of the County Court the last preceding Registry List on file in his office, and by himself and his deputies, during the week commencing on said first Monday in said month, enter on his Registration List the name of any qualified voter whose name is not on said list, on such voter appearing and taking the following oath or affirmation:

TERRITORY OF UTAH, } ss.
COUNTY OF .... }

I.............., being first duly sworn, (or affirmed) depose and say, that I am over twenty-one years of age, and have resided in the Territory of Utah for six months, and in the precinct of..... .... one month immediately preceding the date hereof, and (if a male) am a native born or naturalized (as the case may be) citizen of the United States, and a tax-payer in this Territory; (or if a female), I am native born, or naturalized, or the wife, widow, or daughter (as the case may be), of a native born or naturalized citizen of the United States; and I do further solemnly swear (or affirm) that I am not a bigamist nor a polygamist; that I have not violated the laws of the United States prohibiting bigamy or polygamy; that I do not live or cohabit with more than one woman in the marriage relation, nor does any relation exist between me and any woman which has been entered into or continued in violation of the said laws of the United States prohibiting bigamy or polygamy: (and if a woman) that I am not the wife of a polygamist, nor have I entered into any relation with any man in violation of the laws of the United States concerning bigamy or polygamy.

Suscribed and sworn to before me, this....day of.......1883.

....
Registration Officer .... Precinct.

And said Registration Officer, or his deputies, shall strike from said lists the names of all persons who have died or removed from the precinct, also the names of all persons who he has reason to believe have become disqualified to vote under the act of Congress approved March 22nd, A. D. 1882, entitled "An Act to amend Section 5352 of the Revised Statutes of the United States in reference to bigamy, and for other purposes," unless, after being notified in writing, such person shall take and subscribe the oath hereinbefore set forth; *Provided*, That the action of any Registration Officer may be revised and reversed by this Commission upon a proper showing.

RULE III.

Upon the completion of the lists, it shall be the duty of each Registration Officer to prepare triplicate lists in alphabetical order for each precinct containing the names of all registered voters, one of which lists shall be filed in the office of the Clerk of the County Court on or before the first day of July next; one list he shall cause to be posted up in each precinct at least fifteen days before the day of election, at or near the place of election, and the other list shall be transmitted by him to the Judges of Election of the several precincts for use at the polls. And he shall transmit the affidavits of voters to the Secretary of the Commission.

RULE IV.

Voters removing from one election precinct to another in the same county may appear before the Registration Officer at any time previous to the filing of the lists in the office of the Clerk of the County Court, and have their names erased therefrom, and they may thereupon have their names registered in the precinct to which they may remove.

RULE V.

The Registration Officer of each county shall cause to be written or printed a notice which shall designate the office or offices to be filled, and stating that the election will commence at.......... (designating the place for holding the polls), one hour after sunrise, and continue until sunset on the 6th day of August, A. D. 1883.

Dated at................, on this....day of................, A. D. 1883.

....
Registration Officer.

A copy of which shall be posted up at least fifteen days before the election, in the three public places in the precinct best calculated to give notice to all the voters. It shall be the duty of the Registration Officer to give notice on the lists posted as aforesaid, that the Deputy Registration Officer of such precinct will hear objections to the right to vote of any person registered, until sunset on the 6th day preceding the day of election. Said objection shall be made by a qualified voter, in writing, and delivered to said Deputy Registration Officer, who shall issue a written notice to the person objected to, stating the place, day and hour, when the objection shall be heard. The person making the objection shall serve, or cause to be served, said notice on the person objected to, and shall also make return of such service to the Deputy Registration Officer, before whom the objection is to be heard. Upon the hearing of the case, if said officer shall find that the person objected to is not a qualified voter, he shall within three days prior to the election transmit a certified list of all such disqualified persons to the Judges of Election appointed by the Commission; and said Judges shall strike such names from the Registry lists before the opening of the polls.

RULE VI.

The Registration Officer for each county is required as soon as may be, after his appointment, to transmit to the Secretary of the Commission, by mail, at Salt Lake City, the names of tree persons, who are proper and eligible persons to act as Judges of Election in each precinct of the county, for the information of the Commission. If in any precinct any person appointed Judge declines to serve, or fails to appear, the Deputy Registration Officer of the precinct shall, by appointment fill the vacancy, and the person so appointed shall qualify as herein provided. And said Registration Officer shall immediately transmit the oath of the person so appointed, together with the name of the person declining to serve, to the Secretary of the Commission.

RULE VII.

The Registration Officers and their deputies shall hold their offices during the pleasure of this Commission, and shall each, before entering upon the discharge of his duties, take and subscribe an oath in substance that "he will support the Constitution of the United States, and will faithfully and impartially perform the duties of his office as herein defined, and that he is not a bigamist or polygamist.

RULE VIII.

The County Registration Officers and their deputies shall receive compensation as follows: For County Registration Officers, $4 per day; for each Deputy Registration Officer, $3 per day, the compensation to be paid for the time during which said officers have been necessarily employed in the discharge of their duties; and said officers are authorized to administer all oaths required in the registration and conduct of the election.

RULES

ADOPTED BY THE UTAH COMMISSION DEFINING THE DUTIES OF JUDGES OF ELECTION FOR THE ELECTION TO BE HELD ON THE FIRST MONDAY IN AUGUST, 1883.

RULE I.

The Commission will appoint three capable and discreet persons, who are eligible, in each precinct of the several counties to act as Judges of Election, one at least of whom shall be of the political party that was in the minority at the last previous election, if any such party there be in such precinct. The Secretary of the Commission will make out certificates of said appointments, and transmit the same by mail or other safe conveyance to the person so appointed, who, previous to entering upon said office, shall take and subscribe an oath, or affirmation, that they will, well and faithfully, perform all the duties thereof, to the best of their ability, and that they will studiously endeavor to prevent any fraud, deceit, or abuse of any election over which they may preside, and that they are not bigamists or polygamists. It in any precinct any person appointed Judge declines to serve, or fails to appear, the Deputy Registration Officer of the precinct shall, by appointment fill the vacancy, and the person so appointed shall qualify as herein provided. And said Registration Officer shall immediately transmit the oath of the person so appointed, together with the name of the person declining to serve, to the Secretary of the Commission.

RULE II.

The Judges of Election will take the oath of office before any Notary Public, Justice of the Peace, or other officer authorized to administer oaths, and send said oath immediately by mail to the Secretary of the Commission, as an evidence of acceptance of the office.

RULE III.

The Commission will provide the necessary books, blanks, stationery and envelopes for each voting precinct; and the Judges of Election will procure the ballot boxes from the Clerks of the County Courts.

RULE IV.

Before opening the polls, the ballot box shall be carefully and publicly examined by the Judges of Election, who shall satisfy themselves that nothing is therein. It shall then be locked and the key delivered to the presiding Judge; and said ballot box shall not be opened during the election.

RULE V.

At the opening of the polls on the day of election, the Judges of Election for their respective precincts shall designate one of the Judges acting as Clerk, who shall have in custody the Registry of voters, and shall make the entries therein required by law; the other of said Judges acting as Clerk shall write the name of each person voting, and opposite to it the number of the vote. Every voter shall designate on a single ballot, written or printed, the name of the person voted for, with a pertinent designation of the office to be filled, which ballot shall be neatly folded and placed in one of the envelopes hereinbefore provided for, and delivered to the presiding Judge of Election, who shall, in the presence of the voter, on the name of the proposed voter being found on the Registry list, and all challenges to such vote being decided in favor of such voter, deposit it in the ballot box without any mark whatever being placed on such ballot or envelope; otherwise the ballot shall be rejected. Whenever any ballot shall be deposited in the ballot box, the Judge having the Registry list shall write the word "VOTED" opposite the name of the person casting the vote.

RULE VI.

Challenge shall be allowed at the polls for cause, by any qualified voter, and the Judges of the Election, or a majority of them, shall hear and immediately decide upon any challenge that may be made. If the challenge is on account of alleged want of citizenship, and it appears that the voter is a person of foreign birth, he shall not be allowed to vote except on producing his naturalization papers, or proving that such papers have been issued and lost or destroyed. And if the voter, being a person of foreign birth, claims the right to vote by reason of being the wife of a naturalized citizen, or that he, or she, has become a citizen by reason of the naturalization of his or her parents, the Judges shall receive the vote upon satisfactory oral proof, without requiring the production of the naturalization papers of the husband or parents.

RULE VII.

As soon as the polls shall be closed, the Judges of Election shall immediately proceed to canvass the votes cast at such election, and continue without adjournment until completed. And all candidates voted for may be present in person, or by representative, to witness said count. If any envelope contains two or more ballots of the same kind folded together, only one shall be counted.

RULE VIII.

The canvass shall commence by the Judges, who have acted as Clerks of the Election, comparing their respective lists, and ascertaining from said lists the number of votes cast. The box shall then be opened, and the ballots therein taken out and counted by the Judges, and the Judges, acting as Clerks, shall each make a list of all the persons voted for. The presiding Judge shall then proceed to open the ballots and call off therefrom the names of the persons voted for, and the offices they are intended to fill; and the Judges, acting as Clerks, shall take an account of the same upon their lists, and all the ballots shall be returned to the ballot box, and the ballot box shall be locked and securely sealed; and the box with the ballots enclosed shall be preserved by the presiding Judge of the Election for twenty days after the result of the election has been declared by the Commission; and said ballot box, with the ballots enclosed, shall be forwarded to this Commission immediately on being so required by the Commission. If not so required, the ballots shall be destroyed by the presiding Judge of the Election, and the ballot boxes shall be transmitted to the office of the Clerk of the County Court.

RULE IX.

After the canvass shall have been completed, the Judges of Election shall add up and determine the number of votes cast for each person for the several offices, which result shall be placed on the lists made by the Judges acting as Clerks of the Election; and the Judges shall thereupon certify to the same, and shall forward all the lists, securely sealed, by mail, or other safe conveyance, to the Secretary of the Commission, at Salt Lake City, Utah.

RULE X.

The Judges of Election shall open the polls one hour after sunrise, and close at sunset.

RULE XI.

The Judges of Election shall receive compensation as follows: $3 per day for conducting the election, and 30 cents an hour for the time necessarily employed canvassing the votes, and each of said officers are authorized to administer all oaths required in the conduct of the election.

OATH

REQUIRED TO BE TAKEN BY VOTERS UNDER SECTION 1 OF THE ACT OF FEBRUARY 22, 1878. (SESSION LAWS OF UTAH, 1878).

TERRITORY OF UTAH, } ss.
COUNTY OF ....

I................, being first duly sworn, depose and say, that I am over twenty-one years of age, and have resided in the Territory of Utah for six months, and in the precinct of............... one month next preceding the date hereof, and (if a male) am a "native born" or "naturalized" (as the case may be) citizen of the United States, and a tax-payer in this Territory, (or if a female), I am "native born," or "naturalized," or the "wife," "widow," or "daughter," (as the case may be) of a native born or naturalized citizen of the United States.

Subscribed and sworn to before me this..... day of........... A. D. 188..

....
Assessor.

OATH

REQUIRED TO BE TAKEN BY VOTERS UNDER THE RULES ADOPTED THE UTAH COMMISSION.

TERRITORY OF UTAH, }
COUNTY OF .... }

I.............., being first duly sworn, (or affirmed) depose and say, that I am over twenty-one years of age, and have resided in the Territory of Utah for six months, and in the precinct of .... one month immediately preceding the date hereof, and (if a male) am a native born or naturalized (as the case may be) citizen of the United States, and a tax-payer in this Territory, (or if a female), I am native born, or naturalized, or the wife, widow, or daughter, (as the case may be) of a native born, naturalized citizen of the United States; and I do further solemnly swear (or affirm) that I am not a bigamist nor a polygamist; that I have not violated the laws of the United States prohibiting bigamy or polygamy; that I do not live or cohabit with more than one woman in the marriage relation, nor does any relation exist between me and any woman which has been entered into, or continued in violation of the said laws of the United States prohibiting bigamy or polygamy; (and if a woman) that I am not the wife of a polygamist, nor have I entered into any relation with any man in violation of the laws of the United States concerning polygamy and bigamy.

Subcribed and sworn to before me this....day of............ A. D. 188..

....
Registration Officer............Precinct

ORDER

OF THE UTAH COMMISSION, ADOPTED FRIDAY, SEPTEMBER 1, 1882.

Wm. A. C. Bryan, Registration Officer for the County of Juab, having submitted to this Commission the following question for our decision:

"If, in any case, a man has violated the laws of the United States, prohibiting bigamy or polygamy, and is not at the time he may apply to be registered as a voter, actually living with two or more wives, should he, or should he not, be deemed a legal applicant for registration?"

The Commission, after due consideration, make the following order:

That any person, male or female, who, in violation of the Act of Congress, approved July 1st, 1862, (sec. 5352, Revised Statutes, United States), or who, in violation of section 1 of the Act of Congress, approved March 22d, 1882, entitled "An Act to amend Section 5352 of the Revised Statutes of the United States, in reference to bigamy, and for other purposes," has entered into any of the relationships described in section 8 of said last named act, is not a legal voter, and cannot be registered.

And the Secretary of this Commission is directed to communicate this order to Mr. Bryan; and all other Registration Officers will take due notice of this order.

NOTE.—The following is section 8 of said act:

That no polygamist, bigamist, or any person cohabiting with more than one woman, and no woman cohabiting with any of the persons described as aforesaid in this section, in any Territory or other place over which the United States have exclusive jurisdiction, shall be entitled to vote at any election held in any such Territory or other place, or be eligible for election or appointment to or be entitled to hold any office or place of public trust, honor or emolument in, under or for any such Territory or place under the United States.

ORDER

ADOPTED BY THE UTAH COMMISSION, SEPTEMBER 6, 1882.

C. C. Goodwin, Registration Officer for Cache County, having submitted the following question:

"Will you please instruct me as to the voting qualifications of females who came to this country after they had arrived at the age af twenty-one years, and who have failed to comply with the naturalization laws, and who remain unmarried?"

After due consideration ordered: That females who at the time of the naturalization of their parents are over the age of twenty-one years, and who have failed to comply with the naturalization laws, and who remain unmarried, cannot register or vote.

In answer to queries from Registration Officers, in substance as follows:

"Can any person, male or female, who lived in polygamous relations after July 1, 1862, register or vote?"

After due consideration the Commission answer, *No.*

On motion of Mr. Pettigrew,

"Ordered: That the Secretary of this Commission is hereby instructed to notify the various County Registration Officers to return to the Secretary of this Commission, after the registration lists have been prepared, the affidavits subscribed to by persons whose names are on said lists, and the provision of Rule 3, requiring the affidavits to be filed in the office of the Clerk of the County Court is hereby rescinded."

ORDER

OF THE UTAH COMMISSION, ADOPTED SEPTEMBER 11, 1882.

Resolved, That the Secretary is directed to send a circular to each County Registration Officer, requiring him to send to the Secretary a list of six proper and eligible persons for each precinct, three of whom shall belong to each party, from whom the Commission may select the three Judges of Election for each precinct, in pursuance of Rule 6, the Registration Officer to designate the party to which each person on the list belongs.

ORDER

OF THE COMMISSION, ADOPTED OCTOBER 19, 1882.

"That every woman in the Territory (otherwise legally qualified) is entitled to vote at the November election, whether she is a tax-payer or not."

ORDER

OF THE UTAH COMMISSION ADOPTED OCTOBER 28, 1882.

The attention of the Judges of Election to be held November 7th, 1882, is called to the following order adopted by the Commission, October 20th, 1882 :

"In the absence of any statutory provision in regard to a special election to fill a vacancy in the office of Delegate to Congress from this Territory, in pursuance of section 26 of the Revised Statutes of the United States, and no call or proclamation having been made by the Governor; and the Act of Congress commonly known as the Edmunds bill being silent as to the authority of this Commission to call a special election in any case: It is ordered that no canvass or return shall be made of any votes cast for candidates to fill such vacancy. But the Judges of the Election will not refuse to count any ballot for candidates for Delegate to the Forty-eighth Congress, by reason of the same having thereon also the name of a candidate for the vacancy in the Forty-seventh Congress.

ORDER

OF THE COMMISSION, ADOPTED FRIDAY, NOVEMBER 3, 1882.

1. In pursuance of the provisions of section 9 of "An Act to amend section 5352 of the Revised Statutes of the United States, in reference to bigamy, and for other purposes," Elijah Sells, E. P. Ferry, Charles C. Goodwin, William H. Hooper, and W. N. Dusenberry, are hereby appointed a Board of Canvassers to canvass the returns of the election for Delegate to the Forty-eighth Congress.

2. The Commission will fill by appointment all vacancies in said Board that may occur by failure to accept, or from other cause.

3. A majority of said Board of Canvassers will determine all questions coming before them, including the awarding and signing of the certificate of election.

4. Upon a day to be designated by this Commission, said Board of Canvassers will meet at the rooms of the Commission, at the Walker Opera House, in Salt Lake City; and the election returns will be opened under the direction of this Commission; and said Board of Canvassers will proceed to ascertain the number of votes cast for each person for Delegate to the Forty-eighth Congress, and they, or a majority of them, shall give a certificate of election to the person so ascertained to have received the largest number of legal votes; which certificate shall be delivered to such person, and said Board of Canvassers shall report their proceedings and the result to this Commission.

ORDER

OF THE UTAH COMMISSION ADOPTED JUNE 13, 1883.

William Jennings having appeared before the Commission on Monday, June 11th, 1883, and made the following statement:

"I decided not to register last year, but appeared before the Deputy Registrar of the Third Salt Lake City Precinct, on Saturday, June 9th, 1883, and took the oath prescribed by Rule 2 of the rules defining the duties of the Registration Officers, and was duly registered. Subsequently I received notice from the Deputy Registrar that my name had been stricken from the list of voters of said precinct by the direction of Thomas C. Bailey, Registration Officer of Salt Lake County. I entered into a polygamous relation prior to July 1st, 1862, and continued in that relation until about the year 1871, at which date my first wife died, and I have since lived and cohabited with but one wife. I, therefore, claim that I have not entered into any marriage relation in violation of law, and that I am entitled to have my name appear on the list of registered voters of said precinct, and ask that the action of the Registration Officer for said county be reversed, and my name restored to the list of voters of said precinct."

After due consideration by the Commission it is ordered "that said William Jennings is within the meaning of Section 8 of the Act of Congress of March 22d, 1882, disqualified as a voter, and is therefore not entitled to register or vote."

THE AUGUST ELECTION, 1883.

ORDER OF THE COMMISSION.

Report of the Special Committee, and the order of the Commission, adopted June 13, 1883.

SALT LAKE CITY, June 13, 1883.

Alex. Ramsey, Chairman of the Commission:

SIR:—Your Committee appointed on May 7th to examine and report in relation to the offices to be filled at the August election 1883, respectfully report: That there are to be elected members of the Legislative Assembly in all the Legislative Districts of the Territory; and also certain county and precinct officers.

As to those officers who should have been elected at the August election in 1882, we find, that by law, some of them are to be elected for a certain number of years; some for a given term "and until their successors are *qualified*"; and some for a given term and "until their successors are *elected and qualified.*"

In regard to vacancies, and the time and manner of filing them, the local laws are difficult of construction in view of subsequent Congressional legislation. But in deference to the decision of the Supreme Court of Utah, as to vacancies, in the case of Kimball vs. Richards in 1882, sustaining the appointment of the Governor of Utah, we are of the opinion that all offices which should have been filled at the general election in 1882, are to be filled at the next general election in August, 1883, for the unexpired term.

We are further of the opinion that the offices of Territorial Superintendent of District Schools, Territorial Auditor of Public Accounts, Territorial Treasurer, and Commissioners to locate university lands, are under the Organic Act of the Territory of Utah, to be appointed by the Governor with the assent of the Legislative Council, and that the acts of the Legislative Assembly providing for filling those offices by an election of the people, are in conflict with said Organic Act, and are therefor invalid.

Respectfully,

A. B. CARLTON,
G. L. GODFREY,
Committee.

The report was adopted, and the following order made:

"That at the general election to be held on Monday, August 6. 1883, there are to be elected members of the Legislative Assembly in the several Legislative Districts of the Territory, and also certain county and precinct officers. And that all county and precinct offices which should have been filled at the August election, 1882, are to be filled at the August election, 1883, for the unexpired term."

ORDER

OF THE COMMISSION, ADOPTED JUNE 18, 1883.

ORDERED, That there shall be appointed three Judges of Election for each municipal corporation of the Territory of Utah, in which municipal elections are to be held, one of whom shall be designated presiding Judge; provided, that in municipal corporations in which there are more than one election precinct, there shall be appointed three additional Judges for each of said precincts. The presiding Judge of each municipal election shall procure from the office of the Clerk of the County Court, at the expense of the city, a certified copy of the last preceding Registration List of the precinct or precincts in which said municipality is located, and if said lists have not been filed with the County Clerk he shall procure a certified copy from the Registration Officer of the county, and on the day designated by the City Charter he shall proceed to revise said list by erasing therefrom the names of all persons who have died, or removed from the precinct, or who are disqualified under the provisions of the Act of Congress approved March 22, 1882, entitled "An Act to amend Section 5352 of the Revised Statutes of the United States, in reference to bigamy, and for other purposes," and adding thereto the names of persons who are entitled to be registered and to vote; provided, that in said revision a new affidavit will not be required of those already registered, except where there is good reason to believe that the voter has gone into polygamy since the last registration. Said Judges are hereby constituted a Board of Canvassers for said election in their respective municipalities, and shall make returns thereof to the Secretary of the Territory, who is hereby authorized and directed to issue certificates of election to the persons who, being eligible, appear by said returns to have been elected; provided, that in municipal corporations having more than one election precinct the Judges of one of said precincts will be designated to receive the canvass of all the others, and make returns thereof to the Secretary of the Territory, who is hereby authorized to issue certificates of election to the persons who, being eligible, appear by said returns to be elected as heretofore provided.

It is further ordered that the order of October 19, 1882, relating to municipal elections, be and the same is hereby rescinded.

ORDER

OF THE COMMISSION, ADOPTED JULY 2, 1883.

A communication was received from the Hon. John Sharp, Chairman Peoples Territorial Central Committee, was submitted by the Chairman, asking answers to the following questions: "Will voting for, at the next general election in this Territory, candidates for the offices of Territorial Treasurer, Auditor of Public Accounts, Superintendents of District Schools, and Commissioners to locate University Lands, upon the same ballots, with candidates for members of the Legislative Assembly, and County and Precinct offices, invalidate such ballots entirely; or will such ballots be counted for members of the Legsslative Assembly, and for County and Precinct offices, and the voting for candidates for Territorial offices be treated as surplusage?"

After careful consideration by the Commission, ordered: That the Secretary of the Commission is directed to state in reply thereto, "that ballots voted at the coming election (August 6th, 1883) containing the names of candidates for other offices than those designated to be filled by the Commission, will be rejected and not counted for any purpose."

ORDER

OF THE COMMISSION, ADOPTED AUGUST 14, 1883.

1. In pursuance of the provisions of Section 9 of an act entitled "An Act to amend section 5352 of the Revised Statutes of the United States, in reference to bigamy and for other purposes," the following named persons, viz: "Arthur L. Thomas, chairman; O. J. Hollister, H. W. O. Margery, W. W. Riter, and James Dunn, are hereby appointed a board to canvass the returns of the general election held in the Territory of Utah, on the sixth day of August, 1883, said board will convene at the rooms of the Utah Commission at the Walker Opera House in Salt Lake City, Utah, on Tuesday, August 21st, at 10 a. m., when the election returns will be opened in the presence of this Commission, and said board will proceed to ascertain the number of votes cast for each person, and they, or a majority of them, will determine all questions coming before them, including the awarding of certificates of election, and shall certify the result of the canvass to this Commission, and the same shall be entered of record, and Arthur L. Thomas, the Secretary of the Territory and ex-officio Secretary of this Commission, is hereby appointed and authorized to issue certificates of election to each of said persons so ascertained to have been elected.

2. The Commission will fill by appointment all vacancies in said Board of Canvassers, that may occur by failure to accept, or from other causes.

3. The canvass of the returns for members of the Legislative Assembly will be made by this Commission, which will issue certificates of election to those persons who, being eligible for such offices, shall appear to have been lawfully elected.

ORDER

OF THE COMMISSION, ADOPTED AUG. 24, 1883.

WHEREAS it has been brought to the attention of this Board that a candidate voted for, for a County office, and another for the Council of the Legislative Assembly, each having received the highest number of votes for said offices respectively, at the election held on the sixth day of August, 1883, are polygamists. Therefore,

Resolved, That this Commission will meet at their rooms in Salt Lake City, on the fifth day of October next, for the purpose of considering these, and any other cases of like character, that may be presented.

Resolved, further, that charges of ineligibility against any officer elect must be submitted in writing, and sworn to, (either positively or from information and belief,) and be filed with the Secretary of the Commission, on or before the 15th day of September, 1883, who will notify the complaining party, and the accused party, to appear before the Commission, at the time and place to be designated, and adduce their evidence.

The Secretary is required to publish this order in the principal newspapers of the Territory.

POPULATION BY COUNTIES AND NATIVITY.

| COUNTIES. | Total. | Native. ||||||
		Born in the Territory.	New York.	Illinois.	Pennsylvania.	Iowa.	Missouri.
Beaver	2814	2002	149	91	57	31	43
Box Elder	4715	3817	140	122	74	103	79
Cache	8365	7403	115	143	71	88	63
Davis	3912	3397	90	83	38	50	39
Emery	427	346	9	11	6	11	5
Iron	3203	2779	56	73	23	58	48
Juab	2473	2109	47	42	21	31	35
Kane	2695	2226	63	52	20	43	33
Millard	2789	2348	62	68	25	41	44
Morgan	1263	1054	23	25	37	26	14
Piute	1339	1065	34	44	19	18	33
Rich	934	699	13	13	13	19	11
Salt Lake	20274	15788	772	415	539	233	257
San Juan	109	150	4	3	2		1
Sanpete	7438	6761	61	134	44	74	88
Sevier	3163	2710	38	83	30	68	23
Summit	3254	2338	220	91	84	45	53
Tooele	3198	2602	89	88	56	49	51
Uintah	707	421	40	15	12	24	29
Utah	12988	10977	242	282	186	303	115
Wasatch	2134	1755	35	77	27	66	13
Washington	3202	2295	147	75	62	37	55
Weber	8510	6675	266	200	182	184	92

POPULATION BY COUNTIES AND NATIVITY.

COUNTIES.	Total.	British America.	England and Wales.	Ireland.	Scotland.	German Empire.	France.	Sweden and Norway.
				Foreign Born.				
Beaver	1104	47	621	143	84	61	6	27
Box Elder	2046	46	644	51	77	48	5	164
Cache	4197	55	1639	15	361	79	5	667
Davis	1367	45	1155	4	85	5		25
Emery	129	1	36	3	5		1	15
Iron	810	19	566	15	52	3	3	16
Juab	1001	24	621	31	34	10	2	41
Kane	390	22	212	6	22	3	3	18
Millard	938	28	527	18	48	6		69
Morgan	520	11	292	21	35	13	1	71
Piute	312	24	95	5	11	5		103
Rich	329	11	212	5	43	8	3	13
Salt Lake	11703	245	6992	377	1003	353	33	1260
San Juan	35		28					
Sanpete	4119	27	740	28	93	28		849
Sevier	1294	21	286	10	55	21	2	168
Summit	1667	81	929	195	135	29	11	137
Tooele	1299	33	675	57	146	18	23	263
Uintah	92	7	40	7	11	4		3
Utah	4985	122	2854	93	305	83	12	510
Wasatch	793	14	265	45	153	2	2	131
Washington	1030	57	406	114	79	45	5	42
Weber	3834	96	2209	78	364	61	12	372

THE TERRITORY OF UTAH.

POPULATION BY COUNTIES AND NATIVITY.

	Native.			Foreign.		
	1880	1870	1860	1880	1870	1860
THE TERRITORY	99969	56084	27519	43994	30702	12754
COUNTIES.						
Beaver	2814	1405	545	1104	602	240
Box Elder	4715	2795	970	2046	2060	638
Cache	8365	5121	1676	4197	3108	929
Cedar			440			301
Davis	3912	3010	2195	1367	1449	709
Emery	427			129		
Green River			104			37
Iron	3203	1610	642	810	667	368
Juab	2473	1344	443	1001	690	229
Kane	2695	1292		390	221	
Millard	2789	1974	579	938	779	136
Morgan	1263	1215		520	757	
Piute	1339	54		312	28	
Rich	934	1291		329	664	
Rio Virgin		368			82	
Salt Lake	20274	10894	7372	11703	7443	3923
San Juan	167			35		
San Pete	7438	3890	2295	4119	2896	1520
Sevier	3163			1294	19	
Shambip			95			67
Summit	3254	1448	130	1667	1064	68
Tooele	3198	1350	728	1299	827	280
Uintah	707			92		
Utah	12988	8439	6153	4985	3764	2095
Wasatch	2134	887		793	357	
Washington	3205	2455	588	1030	609	103
Weber	8510	5242	2564	3834	2116	1111

POPULATION BY RACE AND BY COUNTIES.

COUNTIES.	White 1880	White 1870	White 1860	Colored 1880	Colored 1870	Colored 1860	Chinese 1880	Chinese 1870	Chinese 1860	Indian 1880	Indian 1870	Indian 1860
THE TERRITORY	142423	86044	40125	232	118	59	501*	445		807	179	89
Beaver	3828	2005	785	22			28			40	2	
Box Elder	6357	4429	1608	8	19		159	403		237	4	4
Cache	12544	8219	2601	9	5					9	5	
Cedar			741									
Davis	5272	4454	2886	1		10				7	5	8
Emery	555											
Green River			133									8
Iron	3944	2262	1010	14	4					55	15	
Juab	3468	2028	672	2	1		1			4	2	
Kane	3079	1595			1		17			6	7	
Millard	3721	2655	715	1	2					4	87	
Morgan	1766	1970										
Piute	1529	80		2			131			120	2	
Rich	1262	1953								1	2	
Rio Virgin		449									1	50
Salt Lake	31694	18277	11200	133	51	45		39		19	9	9
San Juan	204											
San Pete	11484	6771	3866	2			67			71	15	
Sevier	4455	19					10			2		
Shambip			162									
Summit	4845	2467	198	7	4		2			2	2	8
Tooele	4330	2177	1000	5			53			152		
Uintah	780			1			33			18		
Utah	17942	12185	8243	6	6	4				25	12	1
Wasatch	2918	1244		1						6		
Washington	4155	3052	691	1	4					26	8	
Weber	12291	7833	3674	17	21			3		3	1	1

SCHOOL, MILITARY AND CITIZENSHIP, AGES, ETC.

	All Ages.			5 to 17 both inclusive.		18 to 44 both inclusive.	21 and over.
	Total.	Male.	Female.	Male.	Female.	Male.	Male.
THE TERRITORY	143963	74509	69454	24468	23599	26480	32773
COUNTIES.							
Beaver	3918	2372	1546	534	534	1223	1407
Box Elder	6761	3585	3176	1188	1038	1367	1622
Cache	12562	6272	6290	2322	2309	1881	2423
Davis	5279	2673	2606	972	945	809	1014
Emery	556	314	242	78	75	150	152
Iron	4013	2031	1982	724	723	672	782
Juab	3474	1810	1664	651	555	597	741
Kane	3085	1595	1490	620	530	488	566
Millard	3727	1909	1818	657	641	654	807
Morgan	1783	962	821	344	314	296	383
Piute	1651	893	758	271	273	365	403
Rich	1263	665	598	226	203	234	260
Salt Lake	31977	16097	15880	4880	4853	6131	7699
San Juan	204	104	100	19	35	54	56
Sanpete	11557	5771	5786	2117	2099	1674	2251
Sevier	4457	2318	2139	835	758	721	876
Summit	4921	2840	2081	748	713	1319	1496
Tooele	4497	2502	1995	785	681	927	1188
Uintah	799	480	319	121	106	244	255
Utah	17973	9009	8964	3144	3131	2904	3700
Wasatch	2927	1555	1372	547	494	531	633
Washington	4235	2356	1879	599	576	1005	1269
Weber	12344	6396	5948	2086	2009	2234	2790

AGES OF NATIVE AND FOREIGN BORN POPULATION.

Years of Age.	Aggregate.	Native White Males.	Native White Females.	Foreign born White Females.	Foreign born White Males.	Colored Males (Including Chinese, Japanese and Indians.)	Color'd Females (Including Chinese, Japanese and Indians.)
Total	143963	51651	47307	21639	21826	1032	508
Under 1 Year	5551	2795	2716	11	8	12	9
1 "	5009	2503	2457	22	13	10	4
2 "	5290	2694	2483	37	37	23	16
3 "	4837	2402	2298	65	55	9	8
4 "	4904	2386	2372	59	62	13	12
5 "	4549	2245	2099	90	95	9	11
6 "	4538	2257	2078	83	93	16	11
7 "	4037	1919	1867	128	112	7	4
8 "	4242	2008	1926	135	137	17	19
9 "	3812	1842	1667	145	146	4	8
10 "	4091	1891	1799	188	169	23	21
11 "	3374	1569	1476	150	172	4	3
12 "	3695	1643	1582	220	217	15	18
13 "	3197	1414	1342	218	204	9	10
14 "	3501	1487	1517	243	234	9	11
15 "	3112	1327	1267	246	248	13	11
16 "	3043	1187	1266	282	275	20	13
17 "	2872	1115	1150	286	305	11	5
18 "	2837	1092	1056	328	306	37	18
19 "	2864	1042	1116	365	312	22	7
20 "	2969	1038	1051	457	343	54	26
21 "	2692	1062	894	376	338	18	4
22 "	2789	1010	902	427	408	25	17
23 "	2341	807	772	364	372	20	6
24 "	2250	720	665	386	443	23	13
25 "	2257	648	582	469	483	54	21
26 "	2113	610	490	478	498	31	6
27 "	1941	557	392	468	502	19	3
28 "	2042	533	435	473	552	36	13
29 "	1560	377	286	416	458	16	7
30 "	2221	551	382	560	631	75	22
31 "	1386	345	250	369	409	13	0
32 "	1642	381	255	473	500	26	7
33 "	1446	309	228	470	418	19	2
34 "	1384	335	178	393	453	22	3
35 "	1676	335	201	514	559	47	20
36 "	1537	318	213	494	478	26	8
37 "	1222	237	175	388	411	10	1
38 "	1383	278	174	444	465	18	4
39 "	1204	240	188	377	392	6	1
40 "	1891	361	231	588	644	41	26
41 "	940	179	130	327	297	6	1
42 "	1216	228	160	437	379	10	2
43 "	1069	208	141	363	351	5	1
44 "	1078	227	134	345	359	12	1
45 "	1297	223	134	403	505	22	10
46 "	1009	201	125	321	351	7	4
47 "	983	194	101	329	355	2	2
48 "	1012	168	116	339	386	3	0

AGES OF NATIVE AND FOREIGN BORN POPULATION.—(Continued.)

Years of Age.	Aggregate.	Native White Males.	Native White Females.	Foreign born White Females.	Foreign born White Males.	Colored Males (Including Chinese, Japanese and Indians.	Color'd Female (Including Chinese, Japanese and Indians
49 Years.	940	139	113	335	349	4	0
50 "	1352	192	144	458	524	23	11
51 "	673	94	80	251	244	3	1
52 "	862	138	85	332	304	2	1
53 "	776	109	76	283	307	1	0
54 "	798	97	77	320	301	2	1
55 "	793	94	68	321	299	8	3
56 "	780	94	90	298	293	2	3
57 "	639	75	64	257	241	0	2
58 "	675	83	54	281	256	0	1
59 "	544	63	63	207	209	1	1
60 "	937	97	78	343	385	14	20
61 "	470	66	46	169	189	0	0
62 "	543	71	51	210	210	1	0
63 "	481	59	61	172	188	0	1
64 "	504	73	57	187	186	1	0
65 "	538	59	56	204	204	9	6
66 "	430	58	53	177	142	0	0
67 "	331	48	43	142	98	0	0
68 "	323	38	51	123	107	3	1
69 "	297	33	37	120	107	0	0
70 "	374	55	47	142	122	5	3
71 "	196	33	31	73	58	1	0
72 "	252	42	39	97	74	0	0
73 "	233	51	31	72	79	0	0
74 "	190	26	26	84	54	0	0
75 "	223	35	29	92	66	0	1
76 "	175	30	19	69	56	1	0
77 "	135	17	25	49	44	0	0
78 "	118	14	17	49	38	0	0
79 "	99	11	17	32	39	0	0
80 and over.	377	59	60	141	113	2	2

NATIVE AND FOREIGN BORN POPULATION.

COUNTIES.	Total.	All Ages.		Native Born.	Foreign Born.
		Male.	Female.		
Beaver	3918	2372	1546	2814	1104
Box Elder	6761	3585	3176	4715	2046
Cache	12562	6272	6290	8365	4197
Davis	5279	2673	2606	3912	1367
Emery	556	314	242	427	129
Iron	4013	2031	1982	3203	810
Juab	3474	1810	1664	2473	1001
Kane	3085	1505	1490	2695	390
Millard	3727	1909	1818	2789	938
Morgan	1783	962	821	1263	520
Piute	1651	893	758	1339	372
Rich	1263	665	598	934	329
Salt Lake	31977	16097	15880	20274	11703
San Juan	204	104	100	169	35
Sanpete	11557	5771	5786	7438	4119
Sevier	4457	2318	2139	3163	1294
Summit	4921	2840	2081	3254	1667
Tooele	4497	2502	1995	3198	1299
Uintah	799	480	319	709	92
Utah	17973	9009	8964	12988	4985
Wasatch	2927	1555	1372	2134	793
Washington	4235	2356	1879	3205	1030
Weber	12341	6326	5948	8510	3834

POPULATION OF MINOR CIVIL DIVISIONS.

BEAVER COUNTY.

PRECINCT.	1880
Adamsville	192
Beaver, (including Beaver City)	1911
Beaver City	1732
Grampion	601
Greenville	214
Minersville	487
Star	313

BOX ELDER COUNTY.

PRECINCT.	
Bear River (coextensive in 1880)	340
Box Elder (incl. Brigham City)	2184
Brigham City	1877
Cal's Fort	350
Curlew	197
Deweyville	539
Grouse Creek	267
Kalton	183
Malad (incl. Corinne City)	577
Corinne City	277
Mantua	356
Park Valley	275
Plymouth	300
Portage	464
Promontory	131
Terrace	251
Willard (incl. Willard City)	749
Will rd City	412

CACHE COUNTY.

PRECINCT	
Benson	181
Clarkston, and Clarkston Village (coext nsiv)	464
Hyde Park, and Hyde Park Village (c ex)	423
Hyrum. and Hyrum Village (co ex.)	1234
Lewiston	525
Logan, and Logan City (coex)	339
Mendon, and Mendon City (coex)	513
Millvale, and Millvale Village (coex)	529
Newton, and Newton Village (coex.)	304
Paradise, an t Paradise City ('oex.)	512
Petersboro, and Petersboro Village (coex.)	76
Providence, and Providence Village (coex)	578
Richmond, and Richmond City (coex)	1198
Smithfield, and Smithfield City (coex)	1179
Trenton	209
Wellsville, and Wellsville City (coex)	1193

DAVIS COUNTY.

PRECINCT.	
Bountiful, South and West	1676
Centreville	529
Farmington	1073
Hooper	332
Kaysville (incl. Kaysville City)	1430
Kaysville City	1187
South Weber	230

EMERY COUNTY.

	1880
(Details cannot be given, as the precincts were not separately returned).	

IRON COUNTY.

PRECINCT.	
Cannonville, and Cannonville Village (coex.)	137
Cedar City (incl.)	892
Cedar City	691
Escalante, and Escalante Village (coex)	623
Hillsdale, and Hillsdale Village (coex.)	179
Panguitch	846
Parago ah, and Paragoonah Town (coex.)	256
Parowan, and Parowan City (ocx.)	957
Summit Creek, and Summit Creek Town (coex)	123

JUAB COUNTY.

PRECINCT.	
Levan	624
Mona	503
Nephi, and Nephi City (coex)	1797
Tintic	550

KANE COUNTY.

PRECINCT.	
Bellevue	58
Duncan's Retreat	79
Glendale	338
Grafton. and Grafton Village (coex)	71
Harmony	150
Johnson	87
Kanab, and Kanab Town (coex)	594
Kanara	174
Mount Carmel	137
Orderville, and Orderville Town (coex.)	514
Pareah	94
Rockville	232
Shunesburg, and Shunesburg Town (coex.)	82
Springdale, and Spring'a'e Town (coex)	50
Toquerville, and Toquerville T wn (coex.)	371
Virgin City	254

MILLARD COUNTY.

PRECINCT.	
Deseret	617
Fillmore, and Fillmore City (coex.)	987
Holden, and Holden Town (coex.)	255
Kanosh	636
Leamington	142
Meadow, and Meadow Town (coex.)	212
Oak Creek	184
Scipio	574

THE TERRITORY OF UTAH.

POPULATION OF MINOR CIVIL DIVISIONS.

MORGAN COUNTY.	1880
PRECINCT.	
Croydon	248
Kenyon	417
Milton	235
Morgan City (incl. Morgan City)	582
Morgan City	433
Peterson	301

PIUTE COUNTY.	
PRECINCT.	
Circleville	416
Fremont	424
Greenwich	514
Marysvale	297

RICH COUNTY.	
PRECINCT.	
Garden City	161
Laketown	239
Meadowville	119
Randolph	446
Woodruff	268

SALT LAKE COUNTY.	
PRECINCT.	
Big Cottonwood	661
Bingham	1022
Brighton	387
Butler	165
Draper	455
East Mill Creek	371
Farmers	320
Fort Douglas	403
Fort Harriman	342
Granger	145
Granite	259
Little Cottonwood	500
Mill Creek	1416
Mountain Dell	95
North Jordan	282
Pleasant Green	179
Salt Lake City	20768
1st Ward	520
2d "	273
3d "	477
4th "	391
5th "	340
6th "	582
7th "	1216
8th "	897
9th "	671
10th "	985
11th "	1327
12th "	1230
13th "	1850
14th "	1863
15th "	1253
16th "	1479
17th "	1133
18th "	617
19th "	1565
20th "	1112
21st "	1027

SALT LAKE COUNTY. (Continued.)	1880
PRECINCT.	
Sandy	488
Silver	121
South Cottonwood	1288
South Jordan	440
Sugar House	738
Union	464
West Jordan	857

SAN JUAN.	
PRECINCT.	
Bluff City	107
Remainder of County	97

SAN PETE COUNTY.	
PRECINCT.	
Chester	188
Ephraim (incl. Ephraim City)	1764
Ephraim City	1698
Fairview (incl. Fairview City)	1014
Fairview City	863
Fayette	278
Freedom	102
Fountain Green	881
Gunnison	729
Manti (incl. Manti City)	1801
Manti City	1748
Mayfield	330
Moroni, and Moroni City (coex)	838
Mount Pleasant, and Mount Pleasant City (coex.)	2004
Petty	216
Spring, and Spring City (coex.)	989
Thistle	117
Wales	306

SEVIER COUNTY.	
PRECINCT.	
Annabella	205
Burrville	203
Central	190
Elsinore	223
Glenwood	462
Joseph	370
Monroe	744
Redmond	156
Richfield, and Richfield City (coex)	1197
Salina	438
Vermillion	112
Willow Bend	146

SUMMIT COUNTY.	
PRECINCT.	
Coalville, and Coalville City (coex.)	911
Echo	245
Hoytsville	281
Henneferville, and Henneferville Town (coex.)	262
Kamas	564

THE TERRITORY OF UTAH.

POPULATION OF MINOR CIVIL DIVISIONS.

SUMMIT COUNTY. (Continued.)	1880
PRECINCT.	
Park City (incl. Park City)	1591
Park City	1542
Parleys Park	200
Peoa	238
Rockport	127
Upton, and Upton Village (coex.)	174
Wanship	538

TOOELE COUNTY.	
PRECINCT.	
Batesville	115
Clover	346
Deep Creek	174
Grantsville (incl. Grantsville City)	12 5
Grantsville City	1067
Jacob City	125
Lake View	121
Mill	177
Ophir	592
Stockton	515
Tooele (incl. Tooele City)	1006
Tooele City	918
Vernon	181

UINTAH COUNTY.	
PRECINCT.	
Ashley	799

UTAH COUNTY.	
PRECINCT.	
Alpine, and Alpine City (coex.)	319
American Fork (incl. American Fork City)	1825
American Fork City	1299
Benjamin	150
Cedar Fort	250
Fairfield	172
Goshen	645
Lehi (incl. Lehi City)	1538
Lehi City	1420
Payson, and Payson City (coex.)	1788
Pleasant Grove, and Pleasant Grove City (coex.)	1775
Provo, and Provo City (coex.)	3432
Salem	510
Santaquin	715
Spanish Fork, and Spanish Fork City (coex.)	2304
Spring Lake	157
Springville, and Springville City (coex.)	2312
Thistle Valley	81

WASATCH COUNTY.	1880
PRECINCT.	
Charleston	246
Heber, (incl. Heber City)	1616
Heber City	1291
Midway	718
Wallsburg	347

WASHINGTON COUNTY.	
PRECINCT.	
Gunlock	156
Harrisburg and Leeds	334
Hebron	110
Pine Valley	234
Pinto	155
Price, (incl. Price City)	85
Saint George, (incl. Saint George City)	1384
Saint George City	1332
Santa Clara	194
Silver Reef, and Silver Reef City (coex.)	1046
Washington (incl. Washington City)	537
Washington City	483

WEBER COUNTY.	
PRECINCT.	
Eden	329
Harrisville	582
Hooper, and Hooper City (coex.)	849
Huntsville	819
Lynne (incl. part of Ogden City)	873
Ogden City (part of)	823
Marriott	243
North Ogden	956
Ogden City, and part of Ogden City (coex.)	5246
Plain City	653
Riverdale	272
Slaterville	328
Uintah	247
West Weber	603
Wilson	344
Ogden City (in Lynne and Ogden City)	6069
1st Ward	350
2d "	1690
3d "	1311
4th "	2718

TABLE

Showing the number of Names stricken from the Registration Lists during the week ending September 7, 1882, so far as reported.

BEAVER COUNTY.	No. Disfran'd.	No. Removed.	No. Died.	Additional No. Disfran'd.	EMERY COUNTY.	No. Disfran'd.	No. Removed.	No. Died.	Additional No. Disfran'd.
PRECINCT.					PRECINCT.				
Adamsville	5	6	1		Castle Dale				
Minersville	81	10	2		Huntington				
Greenville	12	10	2		Ferron				
Beaver	80	100	10		Moab				
Grampion	20	250	10	20	Price				
Star		72	2		Schofield				
BOX ELDER COUNTY.					GARFIELD COUNTY.				
PRECINCT.					PRECINCT.				
Promontory	1	2			Cannonville				
Malad	1	32	2		Escalante				
Deweyville	16	13			Hillsdale				
Kelton		13			Panguitch				
Terrace		23	2						
Willard	61	27	6	3	IRON COUNTY.				
Plymouth	4	7							
Calls Fort	22	5	2		PRECINCT.				
Mantua	18	2	1	1					
Bear River City	18				Cedar City	51		1	3
Grouse Creek	9	4		5	Kanarrah				
Portage	37	19	1		Summit				
Park Valley	3	4	1	1	Parowan	66	14		
Snowville					Paragoonah				
Brigham	33	50							
CACHE COUNTY.					JUAB COUNTY.				
PRECINCT.					PRECINCT.				
Mendon					Nephi	102	17	4	
Providence	36			50	Mono	19	6		
Benson	29	1	1		Levan	24	34	4	
Richmond	85	10	5		Tintic	2	59		
Clarkston	15	2	2						
Newton					KANE COUNTY.				
Lewiston	21		1						
Logan	260	27	8		PRECINCT.				
Hyde Park	54		1						
Smithfield	120	5	15	30	Moufft Carmel				
Trenton	11	2	2		Glendale				
Wellsville	109	4	6		Johnson				
Hyrum	157		1		Orderville				
Paradise	20	5	1		Kanab				
Peterboro	6				Pahreah	6	16		
Millville	27	18	4						
DAVIS COUNTY.					MILLARD COUNTY.				
PRECINCT.					PRECINCT.				
East Bountiful	113	52	12		Deseret				
West Bountiful	30	16	3	9	Leamington				
South Bountiful	59	9	15	22	Fillmore				
Kaysville	112	42	14		Meadow				
Farmington	79	58	9	38	Kanosh				
Centreville	44	19	4	3	Oak Creek				
South Weber					Scipio				
South Hooper	10	52	1		Holden				

THE TERRITORY OF UTAH.   55

TABLE
Showing the number of Names stricken from the Registration Lists during the week ending September 7, 1882, so far as reported.

MORGAN COUNTY.	No. Disfran'd.	No. Removed.	No. Died.	Additional No. Disfran'd.	SUMMIT COUNTY.	No. Disfran'd.	No. Removed.	No. Died.	Additional No. Disfran'd.
PRECINCT.					PRECINCT.				
Croyden	9	3	2	3	Echo	3			
Morgan	33	13	2	6	Park City				
Milton	18	8	2	3	Snyderville	15	8	1	
Canyon Creek	28	17	4	3	Upton	1	4	3	
Peterson	17	17	2	2	Wanship	11	11		
					Henneferville	14	6		
PIUTE COUNTY.					Coalville	33	17	3	
					Hoytsville	10	11	1	
PRECINCT.					Kamas	20	7	1	
Bullion					Peoa		5	1	
					Rockport	6	2		
RICH COUNTY.					SALT LAKE COUNTY.				
PRECINCT.					PRECINCT.				
Randolph	18	14		4	1st Salt Lake City				
Meadowville	4	9			2d " " "				
Laketown	12	6			3d " " "	535	24	18	
Woodruff	14	9		2	4th " " "				
Garden City					5th " " "				
SAN JUAN COUNTY.					Sandy	11	10		3
					Mill Creek	134	27	8	
PRECINCT.					South Cottonwood	83	37	11	84
Bluff City					Hunter	1			
Montezuma					Mountain Dell	5	4	1	
					Little Cottonwood		30	4	
SAN PETE COUNTY.					South Jordan				
					Bingham				
PRECINCT.					West Jordan	61	37	4	
Mount Pleasant	225	40	8	25	Ugar House	44	43	4	
Ephraim	40	4			Union				
Mono	137	20	7	75	North Jordan	27	4	4	
Manti	15	10	5		Granite				
Petty	32	15	2		Farmers				
Mayfield	37	8	2	6	Silver				
Gunnison	52	29	3		Butler	15	2		
Fayette	38	8		3	Big Cottonwood	30	100	2	30
Chester	24	20			Granger	5	4	1	
Moroni	89	8	2	10	Brighton	15	4	2	
Wales	10	1			Draper				
Fountain Green	44	70	3		North Point	8	2	2	
Fairview	64	55	3		Pleasant Green	2	12	3	
Thistle	21				Fort Herriman				
					East Mill Creek	23	14	1	
SEVIER COUNTY					Riverton	10	4	1	
PRECINCT.					TOOELE COUNTY.				
Aurora					PRECINCT.				
Annabella					Tooele				
Burrville					Stockton	64	17	3	1
Central	No Return.	No Return.			Ophir		8		1
Elsinore					Vernon	4	38	1	3
Glenwood					Clover (St. Johns)	3			
Joseph					Lake View	13	80	1	
Monroe					Batesville	5	17		
Redmond					Mill	11	10		
Richfield					Grantsville	4	15	1	
Salina					Deep Creek	60	70	4	
Vermillion					Quincy				

TABLE

Showing the number of Names stricken from the Registration Lists during the week ending September 7, 1882, so far as reported.

UINTAH COUNTY.	No. Disfran'd.	No. Removed.	No. Died.	Additional No. Disfran'd.	WASHINGTON CO.	No. Disfran'd.	No. Removed.	No. Died.	Additional No. Disfran'd
PRECINCT.					PRECINCT.				
Ashley Fork	35	16	2		Pinto	21	17	2	
					St. George				
UTAH COUNTY.					Harmony	19	7	2	
					Washington	83	12	3	
					Silver Reef	15	188	10	
PRECINCT.					Toquerville	23	15		
Payson	125	40	26		Leeds	25	8	2	
Pleasant Grove					Santa Clara	14	12	14	
Lehi	106	5	4		Pine Valley	15	31	3	
American Fork					Price	7	2		
Provo	165	18	7	65	Gunlock	13	8	1	
Santaquin	30	8	2	20	Grafton	5	1		
Thistle Creek					Hebron	9	6	1	
Spanish Fork	90		3		Virgin City	9	3	1	
Springville	123	12	8		Duncan's Retreat	5	3		
Alpine	16	2	1		Thunesburg	9	1		
Benjamin	8	6	1		Springdale	5	6	1	
Cedar Fort					Rockville	2	5	2	
Fairfield									
Goshen	22	5	1	17	WEBER COUNTY.				
Salem									
Spring Lake	24	20	1		PRECINCT.				
					Uintah	6	2	3	
WASATCH COUNTY.					Wilson	22	17	1	
					West Weber	28	24	5	
PRECINCT.					North Ogden				
Heber City	76	9	6		Marriott	18	2	4	3
Midway	7	19	1		Slaterville	12	8	4	
Wallsburgh	9	12	4		Eden				
Charleston	11	3		2	Lynne				
					Ogden				
					Plain City	25	4	1	
					Huntsville				
					Hooper	35	5	3	3
					Riverdale	11	4	2	4
					Harrisville				

THE TERRITORY OF UTAH.

REGISTRATION AND ELECTION RETURNS.

BEAVER COUNTY.

PRECINCT.	Registration.			Delegate Vote.			Excess of Registra'n over Vote.
	Males.	Females.	Total.	Caine.	Van Zile.	Total.	
Adamsville............	20	25	45	41	2	43	2
Beaver................	253	208	461	333	70	403	58
Frisco................	221	36	257	9	154	163	103
Greenville............	29	27	56	49	4	53	3
Milford...............	59	18	77	19	35	44	33
Minersville...........	75	55	130	91	21	112	18
Total	657	369	1026	542	286	818	217

BOX ELDER COUNTY.

PRECINCT.	Males.	Females.	Total.	Caine.	Van Zile.	Total.	Excess
Bear River City.......	42	43	85	77	....	77	8
Box Elder.............	219	197	416	360	14	374	42
Call's Fort...........	44	43	87	78	1	79	8
Corinne...............	46	46	92	....	74	74	18
Deweyville............	37	30	67	41	9	50	17
Grouse Creek..........	16	21	37	26	3	29	8
Kelton................	36	8	44	6	13	19	25
Mantua................	43	38	81	76	1	77	4
Park Valley...........	27	17	44	26	0	26	18
Plymouth,.............	10	7	17	14	2	16	1
Portage...............	37	33	70	58	3	61	9
Promontory............	13	10	23	15	2	17	6
Snowville.............	15	16	31	26	....	26	5
Terrace...............	49	25	74	1	37	38	36
Willard...............	83	73	156	141	3	144	12
Total	717	607	1324	945	162	1107	217

CACHE COUNTY.

PRECINCT.	Males.	Females.	Total.	Caine.	Van Zile.	Total.	Excess
Benson................	25	18	43	31	8	39	4
Clarkston.............	43	39	82	73	1	74	8
Hyrum.................	130	105	235	203	5	208	27
Lewiston..............	75	66	141	116	2	118	23
Logan.................	433	347	780	617	48	665	115
Mendon................	80	74	154	140	....	140	14
Milville..............	57	45	102	79	....	79	23
Newton................	22	28	50	46	....	46	4
Providence............	49	49	98	80	1	81	17
Paradise..............	65	59	124	116	....	116	8
Petersboro............	6	6	12	11	....	11	1
Richmond..............	104	90	194	179	2	181	13
Smithfield............	152	121	273	238	3	246	27
Trenton...............	20	14	34	25	4	29	5
Wellsville............	116	111	227	205	1	206	21
Hyde Park.............	37	35	72	67	....	67	5
Total	1414	1207	2621	2226	80	2306	315

DAVIS COUNTY.

PRECINCT.	Registration.			Delegate Vote.			Excess of Registra'n over Vote.
	Males.	Females.	Total.	Caine.	Van Zile.	Total.	
Centerville...	58	58	116	84	12	96	20
East...	120	105	225	185	24	209	16
Farmington...	107	96	203	153	15	168	35
Kaysville...	217	153	370	284	20	304	66
South Weber...	32	23	55	36	17	53	2
South Hooper...	38	45	83	61	12	73	10
South...	59	44	103	91	5	96	7
West...	29	28	57	50	....	50	7
Total...	660	552	1212	944	105	1049	163

EMERY COUNTY.

Castle Dale...	50	37	87	84	....	84	3
Ferron...	48	33	81	68	....	68	13
Huntingdon...	34	25	59	50	....	50	9
Moab...	16	11	27	14	5	19	8
Price...	24	15	39	20	....	20	19
Schofield...	24	3	27	13	10	23	4
Total...	196	124	320	249	15	264	56

GARFIELD COUNTY.

Cannonville...	11	17	28	25	....	25	3
Escalante...	57	41	98	68	....	68	30
Hillsdale...	11	15	26	15	....	15	11
Panguitch...	89	61	150	129	5	134	16
Total...	168	134	302	237	5	242	60

IRON COUNTY.

Cedar City...	90	96	186	157	....	157	29
Kanarra...	26	19	45	44	....	44	1
Parowan...	112	29	141	157	20	177	....
Paragoonah...	36	29	65	57	....	57	8
Summit...	11	11	22	17	2	19	3
Total...	275	184	459	432	22	454	41

JUAB COUNTY.

Levan...	52	47	99	84	5	89	10
Mona...	39	34	73	54	....	54	19
Nephi...	238	210	448	398	8	406	42
Tintic...	118	24	142	2	60	62	80
Total...	447	315	762	538	73	611	151

KANE COUNTY.

PRECINCT.	Registration.			Delegate Vote.			Excess of registrat'n over Vote
	Males.	Females.	Total.	Caine.	Van Zile.	Total.	
Glendale	41	36	77	51	....	51	26
Johnson	6	3	9	6	3	9	0
Kanab	40	28	68	63	1	64	14
Mount Carmel	18	15	33	27	....	27	6
Orderville	30	19	49	44	....	44	5
Pahreah	13	11	24	13	11	24	0
Total	148	112	260	204	15	219	51

MILLARD COUNTY.

PRECINCT.	Males.	Females.	Total.	Caine.	Van Zile.	Total.	Excess
Deseret	58	47	105	81	1	82	23
Fillmore	79	96	175	127	23	150	25
Holden	45	43	88	77	4	81	7
Kanosh	60	50	110	95	6	101	9
Leamington	22	16	38	36	1	37	1
Meadow	31	24	55	47	....	47	8
Oak Creek	16	18	34	28	....	28	6
Scipio	56	57	113	84	10	94	19
Total	367	351	718	575	45	620	98

MORGAN COUNTY.

PRECINCT.	Males.	Females.	Total.	Caine.	Van Zile.	Total.	Excess
Croydon	27	20	47	30	8	38	9
Canyon Creek	57	48	105	89	2	91	14
Milton	36	24	60	41	9	50	10
Morgan	75	60	135	110	12	122	13
Peterson	29	17	46	35	5	40	6
Total	224	169	193	305	36	341	52

PIUTE COUNTY.

PRECINCT.	Males.	Females.	Total.	Caine.	Van Zile.	Total.	Excess
Bullion	80	7	87	7	60	67	20
Circleville	26	17	43	25	4	29	14
Fremont	43	22	65	57	....	57	8
Greenwich	32	23	55	34	2	36	19
Milmont	11	7	18	11	2	13	5
Thurber	32	30	62	42	1	43	19
Total	224	106	330	176	69	245	85

RICH COUNTY.

PRECINCT.	Males.	Females.	Total.	Caine.	Van Zile.	Total.	Excess
Garden City	28	27	55	45	....	45	10
Lake Town	32	23	55	42	....	42	13
Meadowville	11	11	22	18	....	18	4
Randolph	41	38	79	56	3	59	20
Woodruff	36	25	61	43	1	44	17
Total	148	144	272	204	4	208	64

SALT LAKE COUNTY.

PRECINCT.	Registration. Males.	Registration. Females.	Registration. Total.	Delegate Vote. Caine.	Delegate Vote. Van Zile.	Delegate Vote. Total.	Excess of Registra'n over Vote.
Alta	108	8	116	3	64	67	49
Bingham	186	32	218	3	149	152	64
Big Cottonwood	84	73	157	141	3	144	13
Brighton	22	18	40	34	2	36	4
Butler	25	16	41	33	2	35	6
Draper	93	61	154	147	1	148	6
East Mill Creek	42	40	82	78	1	79	3
Farmers	34	30	64	49	5	54	10
Ft. Herriman	68	24	92	49	24	73	19
Granite	25	19	44	30	4	34	10
Granger	31	27	58	44	4	48	10
Hunter	12	10	22	21	....	21	1
Mill Creek	148	126	274	226	11	237	37
Mountain Dell	14	9	23	15	1	16	7
North Jordan	45	40	85	75	4	79	6
North Point	16	16	32	26	2	28	4
Pleasant Green	33	26	59	55	....	55	4
Riverton	23	21	44	42	....	42	2
Sandy	78	61	139	89	20	109	30
South Cottonwood	194	116	310	171	64	235	75
South Jordan	32	25	57	49	1	50	7
Sugar House	63	57	120	95	15	110	10
Silver	18	3	21	1	6	7	14
Salt Lake City	2837	2430	5267	3261	1252	4513	754
Union	54	51	105	80	9	89	16
West Jordan	105	98	203	186	4	190	13
Total	4390	3437	7827	5003	1648	6651	1174

SAN JUAN COUNTY.

PRECINCT.	Males.	Females.	Total.	Caine.	Van Zile.	Total.	Excess
Bluff City	16	22	38	....	....	....	....
Montezuma	4	2	6	....	....	....	....
Total	20	24	44	20	24	44	....

SEVIER COUNTY.

PRECINCT.	Males.	Females.	Total.	Caine.	Van Zile.	Total.	Excess
Anabella	14	10	24	22	1	23	1
Willow Bend	28	18	46	28	....	....	....
Burrville	27	25	52	39	1	40	12
Central	22	16	38	32	....	32	6
Elsinore	33	36	69	55	4	59	10
Glenwood	49	46	95	82	....	82	17
Joseph	40	41	81	48	8	56	25
Monroe	75	59	134	92	23	115	19
Redmond	14	16	30	28	....	28	2
Richfield	91	83	174	126	10	136	38
Salina	56	39	95	69	4	73	22
Vermillion	12	8	20	12	1	13	7
Total	461	397	858	633	52	657	159

THE TERRITORY OF UTAH.

SANPETE COUNTY.

PRECINCT.	Registration.			Delegate Vote.			Excess of Registrat'n over Vote.
	Males.	Females.	Total.	Caine.	Van Zile.	Total.	
Chester................	24	16	40	26	4	30	10
Ephraim...............	150	153	303	247	11	258	55
Fayette................	26	31	57	50	....	50	7
Fairview...............	107	90	197	173	3	176	21
Fountain Green........	69	65	134	120	....	120	14
Gunnison..............	68	63	131	100	12	112	19
Manti.................	196	164	360	294	15	309	51
Mount Pleasant........	195	150	345	252	52	304	45
Mayfield..............	27	22	49	47	....	47	2
Moroni...............	103	86	189	147	6	153	36
Petty.................	29	20	49	28	3	31	18
Spring City...........	94	81	175	125	14	139	36
Thistle...............	12	8	20	16	....	16	4
Wales................	34	23	57	46	3	49	8
Total............	1134	972	2106	1671	123	1794	346

SUMMIT COUNTY.

Coalville.............	133	115	248	197	26	223	25
Echo.................	40	24	64	20	24	44	24
Henneferville.........	42	29	71	64	3	67	4
Kamas................	77	66	143	98	7	105	36
Park City............	659	217	876	29	601	630	246
Peoa.................	39	34	73	69	1	70	3
Rockport.............	15	13	28	22	3	25	3
Parley's Park.........	31	15	46	23	1	24	22
Upton................	27	17	44	34	1	35	9
Wanship.............	45	34	79	61	13	74	5
Hoytsville............	45	33	78	66	4	70	8
Total...........	1153	597	1750	683	684	1367	385

TOOELE COUNTY.

Batesville............	16	11	27	26	....	26	1
Clover...............	34	32	66	59	....	59	7
Deep Creek..........	17	13	30	8	17	25	5
Grantsville...........	104	101	205	183	2	185	20
Lakeview............	20	15	35	30	....	30	5
Mill.................	16	13	29	25	....	25	4
Ophir................	37	16	53	1	31	32	21
Quincy...............	5	5	10	8	1	9	1
Stockton.............	48	36	84	4	51	55	29
Tooele...............	130	133	263	220	21	241	22
Vernon...............	23	18	41	31	1	32	9
Total.............	450	393	843	595	124	719	124

UINTAH COUNTY.

Ashley...............	148	79	227	99	21	120	107

62   THE TERRITORY OF UTAH.

UTAH COUNTY.

PRECINCT.	Registration.			Delegate Vote.			Excess of Registrat'n over Vote.
	Males.	Females.	Total.	Caine.	Van Zile.	Total.	
Alpine	75	44	119	90	11	101	8
American Fork	188	171	359	278	23	301	58
Benjamin	30	22	52	36	10	46	6
Cedar Fort	34	26	60	55	2	57	3
Fairfield	22	16	38	15	9	24	14
Goshen	65	56	121	89	4	93	28
Lehi	213	179	392	324	18	342	50
Payson	253	222	475	420	9	429	46
Pleasant Grove	199	169	368	307	18	325	43
Provo	535	496	1031	712	90	812	219
Salem	51	54	105	87	1	88	17
Santaquin	80	71	151	134	....	134	17
Spanish Fork	294	248	542	474	11	485	57
Springville	278	245	523	351	67	418	105
Spring Lake	12	11	23	9	3	12	11
Thistle	54	14	68	22	2	24	44
Total	2383	2044	4427	3403	278	3691	726

WASHINGTON COUNTY.

Duncan's Retreat	42	35	77	10	....	10	67
Gunlock	9	7	15	12	....	12	4
Grafton	9	8	17	19	....	19	...9
Harmony	8	9	17	14	....	14	3
Hebron	12	9	21	18	....	18	3
Leeds	40	31	71	5	.7	32	39
Pinto	19	19	38	36	....	36	2
Pine Valley	13	17	30	54	....	....	...
Price	31	25	56	16	....	16	40
Rockville	7	7	14	43	....	43	...
Shonesburgh	8	4	12	15	....	15	...
Springdale	11	6	17	13	....	13	4
Santa Clara	41	23	64	25	....	25	39
Silver Reef	61	49	110	16	209	225	...
St. George	143	133	276	235	2	237	39
Toquerville	241	41	282	64	....	64	218
Virgin City	11	9	20	60	....	60	...
Washington	28	23	51	92	1	93	...
Total	734	455	1188	747	219	932	458

WASATCH COUNTY.

Heber City	182	135	317	231	6	237	80
Midway	74	58	132	117	....	117	15
Wallsburg	47	43	90	71	1	72	8
Charleston	31	20	51	45	1	46	5
Total	334	256	590	464	8	472	108

WEBER COUNTY.

PRECINCT.	Registration.			Delegate Vote.			Excess of Registration over Vote.
	Males.	Females.	Total.	Caine.	Van Zile.	Total.	
Eden................	54	36	90	79	1	80	10
Harrisville..............	66	54	120	98	7	105	15
Hooper....................	103	94	197	159	18	177	20
Huntsville.................	99	80	179	146	20	166	13
Lynne.....................	70	60	130	96	20	116	14
Marriott..................	31	22	53	36	14	50	3
North Ogden........ ...	135	95	230	197	7	204	26
Ogden	1019	791	1810	966	651	1617	193
Plain City................	104	80	184	137	37	174	10
River Dale...............	33	26	59	55	1	56	3
Slaterville	58	41	99	61	35	96	3
Uintah.........	32	30	62	26	20	46	16
West Weber..............	57	65	122	114	1	115	7
Wilson..................	48	40	88	70	9	79	9
Total.....	1909	1514	3423	2240	841	3081	342
	Males.	Females.	Total.	Caine.	Van Zile.	Total.	Scattering
Grand Total.............	18772	14494	33266	23039	4884	27923	12

PRECINCTS NOT RETURNED.

Kane County—Johnson : registration, 9 ; no return. Pahreah : registration, 24 ; no return. Pine Valley : registration, 30 ; no return ; vote, Caine 54, Van Zile, 0.
San Juan County—Bluff City : registration, 38 ; no return. Montezuma : registration, 6 ; no return.
Washington County—Leeds, poll No. 1 :, no return ; registration, 59.

ANALYTICAL TABLE OF THE REGISTRATION AND ELECTION FOR DELEGATE TO CONGRESS.

Counties.	Total Registration.	Males Registered.	Females Registered.	Total Vote.	People's Vote.	Liberal Vote.	People's Majority.	Liberal Majority.	Per cent. of Registered Vote Polled.	Per cent. of votes for People's Candidate.	Per cent. of votes for Liberal Candidate
Beaver	1026	657	369	828	542	286	256		80	65.5	34.5
Box Elder	1324	717	607	1107	945	162	783		83	85.4	14.6
Cache	2622	1415	1207	2306	2226	80	2146		88	96.5	3.5
Davis	1212	660	552	1049	944	105	839		.86	90.	10.
Emery	320	196	124	264	249	15	234		82	94.	6.
Garfield	302	168	134	242	237	5	232		80	97.9	2.1
Iron	528	275	253	454	432	22	410		86	95.2	4.8
Juab	762	447	315	611	538	73	465		80	88.	12.
Kane	270	149	121	186	185	1	184		69	99.45	.55
Millard	718	367	351	620	575	45	530		86	92.7	7.3
Morgan	393	224	169	341	305	36	269		86	89.4	10.6
Piute	330	224	106	245	176	69	107		74	71.8	28.2
Rich	272	148	124	208	204	4	200		76	98.	2.
Salt Lake	7827	4390	3437	6651	5003	1648	3355		85	75.2	24.8
San Juan	44	20	24	31	31		31		70	100.	
Sanpete	2092	1140	952	1794	1671	123	1548		86	93.1	6.9
Sevier	858	461	397	685	633	52	581		80	92.4	7.6
Summit	1748	1153	595	1367	683	684		1	78	49.96	51.04
Tooele	846	450	396	719	595	124	471		85	82.8	17.2
Uintah	227	148	79	120	99	21	78		52	82.5	17.5
Utah	4338	2384	1954	3681	3403	278	3125		84	92.4	7.6
Wasatch	592	336	256	472	464	8	456		80	98.3	1.7
Washington	1192	734	458	917	698	219	533		81	77.4	22.6
Weber	3473	1909	1514	3081	2240	841	1399		90	72.7	27.3
Totals	33266	18772	14494	27979	23078	4901	18233		84	82.5	17.5

[Exhibit "A."]

STATEMENT

Showing the total Number of Registered Voters in the Territory of Utah at the close of the Revision of the Registration Lists on Saturday, June 9th, 1883.

COUNTIES.	Stricken from List.		Death.		Removed.		On Acc't of Polygamy.		Added.		Total on Register.	
	Males	Females	Males	Females	Males	Females	Males	Females	Males	Females	Males	Females
Beaver	81	19	9	1	38	12	5	10	152	69	709	419
Box Elder	34	27	2	1	37	31	6	16	66	30	655	560
Cache	54	33	9	10	40	19	4	4	133	112	1492	1201
Davis	29	18	4	2	25	17	5	3	63	50	684	577
Emery	6	2			10	5			50	35	201	143
Garfield	11	9	1		10	9			30	17	130	99
Iron	43	40	1	3	22	17	1	1	21	32	271	277
Juab	29	17	1	1	28	16			81	24	501	316
Kane	37	27	3	2	32	23	2	1	24	9	116	89
Morgan	9	7	1	1	9	15	1	1	16	15	229	177
Millard	22	27	1	4	21	21	44	32	71	34	347	309
Piute	48	13	2	1	47	11			86	65	298	172
Rich	14	12	2	1	12	9	1	1	35	15	164	116
San Juan		1							15	7	31	27
Salt Lake	135	70	15	9	133	48	3	8	352	216	4839	3387
Sanpete	40	27	6	3	43	23	10	15	145	58	1023	854
Summit	43	19	7	7	55	18	2	1	246	68	1369	632
Sevier	45	35	4	2	43	25	8	2	104	55	522	420
Tooele	36	36	3	3	33	31	2	1	57	21	380	297
Utah	62	53	7	16	47	41	52	80	166	93	2487	2005
Wasatch	18	11			18	12			34	28	315	270
Washington	85	49	9	5	77	44	9	11	65	41	641	407
Weber	96	52	16	4	71	50	4	4	203	165	1998	1583
*Uintah											148	79
	977	604	103	76	851	491	129	191	2215	1274	19596	14425

*No returns of the revisions made during the week ending June 9th, 1883.

BEAVER COUNTY.

PRECINCTS.	Stricken from List. Males	Stricken from List. Females	Death. Males	Death. Females	Removed. Males	Removed. Females	On Acc't of Polygamy. Males	On Acc't of Polygamy. Females	Added. Males	Added. Females	Total on Register. Males	Total on Register. Females
Adamsville	1						1	2	5	2	25	26
Beaver	20	10	3	1	17	9			22	18	259	216
Greenville	2		1		1				1	3	28	50
Grampion	57	9	5		7	3			99	34	253	65
Minersville	1				1		4	8	11	5	82	59
Star					12				14	7	62	23
Total	81	19	9	1	38	12	5	10	152	69	709	410

BOX ELDER COUNTY.

	Stricken Males	Stricken Females	Death Males	Death Females	Removed Males	Removed Females	Polygamy Males	Polygamy Females	Added Males	Added Females	Total Males	Total Females
Bear River City			1		5	1			5	5	46	48
Box Elder	5	4			5	4			9	4	246	205
Calls Fort	9	10	1		8	10			4	3	37	37
Corinne					1	1	3	8			20	15
Curlew	1	1			1	1	3	8	3	1	8	10
Deweyville				1	3	2			3	4	37	31
Grouse Creek									6		22	21
Malad	1	7			1	7			14	11	59	50
Mantua	2	2			2	2			2	1	43	38
Plymouth									3	1	15	8
Park Valley	2				2				5	2	29	20
Promontory	3	1			3	1			1	1	11	10
Willard	11	2			11	2			11	6	84	76
Total	34	27	2	1	37	31	6	16	66	39	655	569

CACHE COUNTY.

	Stricken Males	Stricken Females	Death Males	Death Females	Removed Males	Removed Females	Polygamy Males	Polygamy Females	Added Males	Added Females	Total Males	Total Females
Benson	2	1	1		2				5		41	
Clarkston	3	3		1	1	2	1	1	8	7	46	42
Hyrum	1	1			1	1			12	11	140	115
Hyde Park									4	1	41	36
Lewiston	4	5	1	1	1	2	2	2	11	9	86	62
Logan	14	8	2	5	12	3			17	20	462	326
Millville	4	2		2	4				6	9	68	43
Mendon	4	2	1	1	2	2			3	2	82	73
Newton	2	2			1	1	1	1	3	4	24	29
Paradise	7	4	1		7	4			7	4	93	62
Peterboro									1		7	6
Richmond	3	2	2		1	2			16	12	109	107
Smithfield	6				6				20	10	143	104
Trenton									6	2	24	16
Wellsville	4	3			2	2			14	12	126	120
Total	54	33	9	10	40	19	4	4	133	112	1492	1201

DAVIS COUNTY.

	Stricken Males	Stricken Females	Death Males	Death Females	Removed Males	Removed Females	Polygamy Males	Polygamy Females	Added Males	Added Females	Total Males	Total Females
Centreville			1		1	1			5	6	62	62
East Bountiful	6	1	1		5	1	1		6	4	121	108
Farmington	7	5			6	4	1	1	8	7	104	96
Kaysville	13	9	1	2	8	6	1		32	31	227	108
South Weber									2	1	33	25
South Bountiful	1	1			1	1			2	2	56	51
South Hooper			1		2	2			4	3	49	41
West Bountiful	2	2			2	2	2	2	4	5	32	26
Total	29	18	4	2	25	17	5	3	63	50	684	577

THE TERRITORY OF UTAH.

EMERY COUNTY.

PRECINCTS	Stricken From List Males	Stricken From List Females	Death Males	Death Females	Removed Males	Removed Females	On Acc't of Polygamy Males	On Acc't of Polygamy Females	Added Males	Added Females	Total on Register Males	Total on Register Females
Castle Dale									5	6	55	44
Price									12	9	37	23
Huntington					4	3			25	14	59	39
Ferron	6	2			6	2			8	0	50	37
Total	6	2			10	5			50	35	201	143

GARFIELD COUNTY.

	Males	Females	Males	Females	Males	Females	Males	Females	Males	Females	Males	Females
Cannonville	2	1	1		1	1			10	4	20	21
Hillsdale	4	3			4	3			5	3	12	15
Panguitch	5	5			5	5			15	10	98	63
Total	11	9	1		10	9			30	17	130	99

IRON COUNTY.

	Males	Females	Males	Females	Males	Females	Males	Females	Males	Females	Males	Females
Cedar City	10	8			9	7	1	1	5	10	83	98
Parowan	5	6		1	5	5			7	9	114	102
Paragoonah	6	4			6	4				4	30	29
Kanarrah	20	22	1	1					6	6	26	21
Summit	2	2		1	2	1			3	3	24	24
Total	43	40	1	3	22	17	1	1	21	32	277	277

JUAB COUNTY.

	Males	Females	Males	Females	Males	Females	Males	Females	Males	Females	Males	Females
Levan	2	1	1		1	1			14	9	63	55
Mona	4	4			4	4			10	4	41	33
Nephi	4	9		1	4	8			22	8	256	200
Tintic	10	3			19	3			35	3	138	19
Total	20	17	1	1	28	16			81	24	501	316

KANE COUNTY.

	Males	Females	Males	Females	Males	Females	Males	Females	Males	Females	Males	Females
Glendale	17	12	1	1	15	11			11	5	36	27
Kanab	7	7	1	1	6	6			7	2	40	32
Mount Carmel	3	3			4	2			2	1	17	13
Orderville	10	5	1		7	4	2	1	4	1	23	17
Total	37	27	3	2	32	23	2	1	24	9	116	89

MORGAN COUNTY.

	Males	Females	Males	Females	Males	Females	Males	Females	Males	Females	Males	Females
Canyon Creek	1	2			1	1	1		3	3	59	49
Croyden					1	1			3	1	29	20
Morgan	2	3	1	1	1	11			5	8	78	65
Milton	2				2				1	1	35	25
Peterson	4	2			4	2			4	2	28	18
Total	9	7	1	1	9	15	1		16	15	229	177

MILLARD COUNTY.

PRECINCT.	Stricken from List. Males	Stricken from List. Females	Death. Males	Death. Females	Removal. Males	Removal. Females	On Acc't of Polygamy. Males	On Acc't of Polygamy. Females	Added. Males	Added. Females	Total on Register. Males	Total on Register. Females
Deseret................		1		1					16	11	73	57
Fillmore...............	9	9			7	6	2	3	19	6	91	91
Holden................	4	4	1	1	7	7	10	26	5	4	43	41
Leamington...........	2	2			2	2			7	3	24	19
Meadow...............	3	2			3	2			6	2	34	25
Oak Creek............	2	4		1	1	1	1	2	3		17	14
Scipio.................	2	5		1	1	3	1	1	16	8	65	62
Total.................	22	27	1	4	21	21	14	32	71	34	347	309

PIUTE COUNTY.

PRECINCT.	Stricken Males	Stricken Females	Death Males	Death Females	Removal Males	Removal Females	Polygamy Males	Polygamy Females	Added Males	Added Females	Total Males	Total Females
Circleville............		2				2			30	16	57	30
Deer Trail............											15	3
Fremont..............	3	3			3	3			23	20	63	39
Marysvale............	39	4			39	4			5	10	46	13
Greenwich............	2	1	1	1	1				4	4	34	26
Meadowville..........	1	1	1		1				3		12	11
Thurber..............	2	2			2	2			20	15	60	43
Wilmont..............	1				1				1		11	7
Total.................	48	13	2	1	47	11			86	65	298	172

RICH COUNTY.

PRECINCT.	Stricken Males	Stricken Females	Death Males	Death Females	Removal Males	Removal Females	Polygamy Males	Polygamy Females	Added Males	Added Females	Total Males	Total Females
Garden City..........	3	1			3	1			8	3	40	29
Laketown.............	4	2	1		2	1	1	1	3	4	31	25
Randolph.............	2	3	1		2	2			12	7	51	41
Woodruff.............	5	6		1	5	5			12	1	42	21
Total.................	14	12	2	1	12	9	1	1	35	15	164	116

SALT LAKE COUNTY.

PRECINCT.	Stricken Males	Stricken Females	Death Males	Death Females	Removal Males	Removal Females	Polygamy Males	Polygamy Females	Added Males	Added Females	Total Males	Total Females
Big Cottonwood......	2	2			2	2			6	3	93	70
Butler................	10	1	1		9	1			11	8	27	22
Brighton..............		1						1			21	19
Bingham.............	16			2	14				17		218	
Draper...............	6	6		1	7	1			8	11	86	75
East Mill Creek......	1		1						4	2	47	40
Fort Herriman.......	17	2	1	1	16	1			40	5	92	27
Farmers..............	4	2			4	2			10	11	40	30
Granger..............											33	25
Granite...............	4	2			4	2			3	2	24	19
Hunter................									2	1	14	11
Little Cottonwood....	11	1		1	11				2		102	4
Mountain Dell.......	1	1			1	1			1	11	24	
Mill Creek............			1		2	2			9	6	299	
Mill..................							1	4	4	2	21	14
North Jordan........		1		1	1				6	7	51	45
North Point..........		1				1			3	2	19	17
Pleasant Green......	4	4	1		3	4			1	3	34	32
Riverton.............	5	7	1		11				16		26	22
1st Salt Lake City...	4	1	3		1	1			37	36	575	499
2d " " "........	9	7	1		6	5	1		44	23	812	677
3d " " "........				2		1			34	20	561	452
4th " " "........	2	2			2	2			20	19	375	339
5th " " "........	1	1			1	1			35	25	704	538
South Cottonwood...	5	3	1	1	5	2			5	3	194	116
South Jordan........	1	1			1	1			1	3	32	28
Sugar House........	8	3			7	2	1	1	4	3	59	57
Sandy................	10	6		1	10	5			8	5	74	61
Silver................	2	6			2	1			8		24	2
Union................	6	6		1	6	3		2	5		54	44
West Jordan.........	6	8		2	6	6			8	5	104	95
Total.................	135	70	15	9	133	48	3	8	352	216	4839	3387

THE TERRITORY OF UTAH.   69

SAN JUAN COUNTY.

PRECINCTS.	Stricken from List.		Death.		Removed.		On Acc't of Polygamy.		Added.		Total on Register.	
	Males	Females	Males	Females	Males	Females	Males	Females	Males	Females	Males	Females
Bluff		1							15	7	31	27

SANPETE COUNTY.

Chester	5	2	1		4	2			2	3	17	22
Ephraim		1						1	19	7	174	159
Fairview	1	2			1	1	1		9	5	130	80
Fountain Green	2	3			5				15		73	71
Fayette		2		1		1	8	14	11	3	37	33
Gunnison					3	2			19		84	61
Mayfield									9	7	36	29
Moroni	6	5			5	5			5	14	102	96
Mount Pleasant	10	5	1	1	8	5			23	11	190	163
Petty	4	3			4	3			8	1	37	21
Spring	10	4	2	1	8	2	1		14	7	99	83
Thistle					3	2					8	7
Wales	2		1		2				11		36	29
Total	40	27	6	3	43	23	10	15	145	58	1023	854

SUMMIT COUNTY.

Coalville					15	7			36	20	169	135
Echo	12	2		1	12	1			7	6	37	27
Henuefer	3	1			3	1			2	2	41	30
Hoytsville	2	2		1	2	1			8	6	50	36
Kamas		2	3	2					14	5	88	64
Park City	11	5	13	2	8	3			142	10	806	219
Peoa					1	1			10	4	48	37
Parley's Park	7	2			7	1	2		9	5	33	18
Rockport	1	1	1	1	1	1			7	1	21	13
Upton	1	1			1	1		1	3	3	29	19
Wanship	6	3	1		5	3			8	3	48	34
Total	43	19	7	7	55	18	2	1	246	65	1399	632

SEVIER COUNTY.

Monroe	3	2			2	1	1	1	14	9	86	66
Elsinore					1	1			2	2	85	37
Annabella									4	3	19	13
Aurora	3	2			3	2			7	4	31	20
Central	2	3			2	3			4	8	24	16
Richfield	2	3	1		1	3			5	3	95	81
Redmond		1		1					10	6	24	21
Gooseberry									16	8	16	8
Vermillion	3	3			2		4		8		13	6
Burrville	3	2	1		2	2			4	4	26	28
Glenwood	8	5			11		2		9		47	42
Joseph	2	2	1		1	2			10	5	57	46
Salina	19	12	1	1	18	11	1	1	11	8	49	35
Total	45	35	4	2	43	25	8	2	104	55	522	420

TOOELE COUNTY.

Batesville	2	1			2	1				1	14	11
Grantsville	4	7	1	1	3	6			7	5	108	99
Lake View	5	2			5	2	2	1	2	1	18	13
Ophir	8	4	1		7	2			18	2	47	17
Stockton	13	11			13	11			8	5	43	30
Tooele	4	11	1	2	3	9			22	7	150	127
Total	36	36	3	3	33	31	2	1	57	21	380	297

THE TERRITORY OF UTAH.

UTAH COUNTY.

PRECINCT.	Stricken from List. Males	Stricken from List. Females	Death. Males	Death. Females	Removal. Males	Removal. Females	On Acc't of Polygamy. Males	On Acc't of Polygamy. Females	Added. Males	Added. Females	Total on Register. Males	Total on Register. Females
American Fork	2	3		3	1		47	6	1	9	155	200
Alpine	6	3			5	2	1	1	5	6	74	47
Benjamin	1	2			1				3		32	20
Cedar Fort	2	2			2					2	31	25
Fairfield	2	2			1	1			4	3	24	17
Goshen	4	4			3		1	1	2	3	62	55
Lehi	7	9	1		4		2	6	21	12	227	181
Pleasant Grove				3	4	5	1	2	4	8	195	161
Payson	6	1							4	6	261	217
Provo	7	14	3	7	4	7			26	8	548	408
Santaquin									5	1	84	73
Spring Lake	6	5			6	5			4	4	11	10
Springville	7	3	2	1	5	2			58	23	328	271
Salem		1				1			1	8	62	61
Spanish Fork	8	5	1	2	7	3			11	2	299	244
Thistle	4	2			4	2			7	2	62	·15
Total	62	53	7	16	47	41	52	80	166	93	2497	2005

WASATCH COUNTY.

	Males	Females	Males	Females	Males	Females	Males	Females	Males	Females	Males	Females
Charleston	1				1	1			4	5	29	24
Heber	10	3			10	3			17	5	189	137
Midway	4	6			4	6			9	15	79	67
Wallsburgh	3	2			3	2			4	3	48	42
Total	18	11			18	12			34	28	345	270

WASHINGTON COUNTY.

	Males	Females	Males	Females	Males	Females	Males	Females	Males	Females	Males	Females
Gunlock			1								8	8
Hebron	3	3			1	2			1	2	8	9
Leeds	3	2			3	2	9	11	3		41	22
New Harmony	1	1			1	1			3		10	8
Price	1	1			1	1			4	4	12	10
Pinto		1				1			2	2	21	20
Rockville	5	3	3		2	3			5	1	26	26
St. George	10	11			1	10			14	10	146	135
Santa Clara		2				2			7	5	19	21
Silver Reef	43	10	2	1	41	9			7	1	205	82
Toquerville	5	2	2		3	2			7	7	43	35
Virgin City	7	4	1		6	4			2	1	36	31
Washington	7	9		2	7	7			10	8	63	50
Total	85	49	9	5	77	44	9	11	65	41	641	407

WEBER COUNTY.

	Males	Females	Males	Females	Males	Females	Males	Females	Males	Females	Males	Females
Eden	7	2			7	2			3	7	50	42
Harrisville	11	10	2	2	9	8			17	9	70	54
Hooper City			1						7	6	110	99
Huntsville	14		2	1	2	2	3	4	14	7	106	80
Lynne	12	7	2		10	7			7	6	66	60
Marriott	1				· 1		1		4	2	31	24
North Ogden	6	3	1		5	3			19	18	142	112
Ogden	23	13	3		20	13			87	68	1091	840
Plain City	2	2	1	1					11	10	112	89
Riverdale			1						8	12	9	12
Slaterville	1	1			1	1			5	9	62	49
Uintah	9	8	2		7	8			9	2	31	27
Wilson	4	3			4	3			4	2	48	39
West Weber	6	3	1		5	3			8	2	67	56
Total	96	52	16	4	71	50	4	4	203	165	1998	1583

OFFICIAL RETURNS OF ELECTION, AUG. 6, 1883.

COUNCIL.

DISTRICT—Counties	Cache	Rich				Total
James C. Hamilton....	2070	192				2262

DISTRICT—Counties	Box Elder	Weber				Total
F. S. Richards	835	2130				2965
M. H. Beardsley		1				1
Dick Delaney........		1				1
James Horrocks......		1				1

DISTRICT—Counties	Wasatch	Uintah	Summit	Morgan		Total
W. W. Cluff..........	424	37	811	796		2068
R. G. Chambers	1	23	7. 8	3		735

DISTRICT—Counties	S. Lake	Davis	Tooele			Total
Heber J. Grant........	4081	792	507			5380
Heber J. Richards ...	4 82	792	507			5381
William W. Taylor....	4077	792	506			5375
Joseph Barton........	4082	789	507			5378
John B. Meridith......		77				77
John Thompson.......		77				77
L. S. Hills	1					1
Parley L. Williams ...	1					1

DISTRICT—Counties	Utah	Juab				Total
Joel Grover...........	2352	529				2881
Jonathan S. Page.....	2355	493				2848
John M ore	6					6
Charles Foote.........	1					1

DISTRICT—Counties	Sanpete	Sevier	Emery			Total
Luther T. Tuttle......	1552	665	146			2363
F. H. Stott............	1					1
Edwin Scott..........	1					1
O. H. Bliss			1			1
D. D. Green......:...			1			1

DISTRICT—Counties	Millard	Beaver	Iron	Piute	Garfield	Total
Robert W. Heyborne..	626	541	388	229	218	2002
Zera Snow............		193				193
R. Burk...............		2				2
L. S. Lyman..........			2			2
Wm. C. McGregor....			1			1

DISTRICT—Counties	Washington	Kane	San Juan			Total
Edwin D. Woolley....	709	170	57			936
John Rider...........		18				18

HOUSE OF REPRESENTATIVES.

DISTRICT—Counties	Cache	Rich				Total
E. F. Cummings, Jr...	2054	192				2246
Joseph Howell.......	2069	154				2223
J. T. Caine, Jr........	3					3
R. Kirkham..........	1					1
James Arnold.........	1					1
George B ugh........	1					1
William M. Crockett..	1					1
W. G. Bearton........	2					2
J. McAlcote, Jr.......	1					1
W. P. Nebeker........		38				38

DISTRICT—Counties.	Box Elder					Total
O. G. Snow...........	836					836

DISTRICT—Counties..	Weber					Total
D. H. Peery	2121					2121
Joseph Stanford.....	2121					2121
J. S. Dee............	1					1
Charles Horn	1					1

DISTRICT—Counties..	Wasatch	Uintah				Total
Abr m Hatch.........	422	51				473

DISTRICT—Counties..	Summit					Total
John Hoyden.........	824					824
D. C. McLaughlin.....	716					716

DISTRICT—Counties..	Morgan	Salt Lake	Davis			Total
James Sharp.........	300	4081	792			5173
John Morgan.........	350	4077	792			5169
John Clark...........	300	4080	792			5172
D. C. Young.........	300	4072	792			5164
Caleb T. Brinton.....	300	4082	792			5174
Samuel Francis.......	209	4081				5172
P. L. Williams.......		336				336
J. C. Morrill..........		333				333
P. M. Denny.........		333				333
C. K. Gilchrist.......		333				333
W. G. Van Horn.....		333				333
Geo. C. Douglas......		332				332

DISTRICT—Counties..	Tooele					Total
Charles L. Anderson..	500					500

DISTRICT—Counties..	Utah	Juab				Total
W. H. Dusenberry....	2359	491				2850
S. R. Thurman.......	2359	493				2852
William Creer........	2360	493				2853
George Webb........	2320	493				2813
R. Hunter...........	20					20
Oscar Hunter........	15					15
William Webb.......	3					3
James Chipman......	1					1

HOUSE OF REPRESENTATIVES.

District—Counties	Sanpete	Sevier	Piute			Total
K. K. Llewllyn	1550	665	146			2361
A. D. Thurber	1552	665	146			2363
August Anderson	1					1
H. P. Jensen	1					1
John H. Stott	3					3
S. H. Gibsen		65				65
E. M. McIntyre			53			53
P. T. Van Zile			2			2
E. D. Sanford			1			1

District—Counties	Millard					Total
Joseph V. Robinson	624					624

District—Counties	Beaver	Piute				Total
P. T. Farnsworth	548	229				777
P. Lochrle	178					178
D. Tyler	1					1
W. E. Nowers	4					4
K. E. Cowdell	2					2

District—Counties	Iron	San Juan	Garfield			Total
John Houston	388	57	218			663
L. S. Lyman	1					1
S. K. Burton	2					2

District—Counties	Washington	Kane				Total
Jno. Rider	769	104				873
John S. Carpenter		2				2
Martin Slack		4				4

BEAVER COUNTY.

COUNTY OFFICERS.	Beaver.	Greenville.	Adamsville.	Minersville.	Grampion.	Star.	Total.
Judge of Probate, unexpired term.							
F. R. Clayton	320	47	44	96	7	19	533
John Ward Christian	17			18	136	32	203
Clerk of the County Court, unexpired term.							
R. Maeser	325	47	44	96	7	19	538
Norman Woodhouse	14			18	135	32	199
One Selectman, unexpired term, two years.							
James McKnight	325	47	44	97	7	19	539
O. S. Carver	9			17	135	31	192
Assessor and Collector, unexpired term.							
Sam'l N. Slaughter	325	47	44	97	8	19	540
John Forgie	7			17	136	32	192
County Recorder, unexpired term.							
D. L. McDonough	316	40	44	98	95	22	615
E. Tolton	21	7		15	49	29	121
Sheriff, unexpired term.							
Wm. Hutchings, Jr	317	47	44	97	8	20	533
James McGarry	16			16	136	29	197
County Treasurer, unexpired term.							
J. H. Skinner	318	46	44	96	7	20	531
C. W. Byram	10	1		16	136	31	194
Coroner, unexpired term.							
Robert Stoney	327	47	44	96	7	20	541
Luther Carter	9			17	136	31	193
County Prosecuting Attorney, unexpired term.							
B. Ferguson	322	47	43	95	7	21	535
T. C. Burns	9			16	135	29	189
One Seleetman.							
Joseph H. Joseph	325	47	44	96	7	16	535
J. D. Williams	10			18	137	35	200
County Surveyor.							
B. Ferguson	319	46	43	95	7	25	535
E. Buettner	10			18	137	26	191
Superintendent of District Schools.							
F. R. Clayton	324	47	44	97	7	19	538
H. W. Morse	11			16	137	29	193

PRECINCTS.	For Justices.	No. of Votes. Full Term.	No. of Votes. Unex. Term.	For Constable.	No. of Votes. Full Term.	No. of Votes. Unex. Term.
Beaver	Caleb C. Baldwin	323		S. M. Messenger	313	
Greenville	J. A. Barton	47		Wm. Edwards	47	
Adamsville	David D. Rees	44		Jno. T. Joseph	44	
Minersville	Wm. Wood, Sr	98		Geo. Baker	91	
Grampion	R. S. Lipscomb	139		Wm. Haynes	123	
"				M. Fitzgerald	38	
Star	F. W. O'Connor	26		Dan'l Mahoney	17	
"	W. G. Taylor	29		A. N. Stoddard	49	

BOX ELDER COUNTY.

COUNTY OFFICERS.	Box Elder.	Bear River.	Curlew.	Call's Fort.	Park Valley.	Kelton.	Malad.	Mantua.	Grouse Creek.	Promontory.	Plymouth.	Willard.	Terrace.	Portage.	Deweyville.	Total.
Judge of Probate, unexpired term. P. F. Madsen	276	76	29	67	34	No Election.	22	69	25	7	8	126	No Election.	58	38	834
Ryan	276	76	29	67	34		1	69	24	7	8	126		58	36	1
Clerk of the County Court, unexpired term. A. H. Snow	275	76	29	67	34		21	69	25	7	8	125		58	38	831
One Selectman, unexpired term, two years. Carl Jensen	276	76	29	67	34		22	69	26	7	8	126		58	38	835
One Selectman. William Lowe	276	76	29	67	34		23	69	27	7	8	126		58	36	836
Assessor, unexpired term. O. G. Snow	276	76	29	67	34		27	69	27	7	8	126		58	36	840
Collector, unexpired term. O. G. Snow	276	76	29	67	34		27	69	24	7	8	126		58	40	840
County Recorder, unexpired term. A. H. Snow	276	76	29	67	34		23	69	25	7	8	126		58	37	833
Nels Madsen, Jr.	275	76	29	67	34		23	69	25	7	8	125		58	36	1
Coroner, unexpired term. M. L. Ensign	276	76	29	67	34		39	69	25	7	8	126		58	38	852
Sheriff, unexpired term. C. C. Loveland	276	76	29	67	34		23	69	25	7	8	126		58	38	836
County Prosecuting Attorney. R. H. Jones	276	76	29	67	34		22	69	25	7	8	126		58	38	834
County Treasurer. Wm. Horsley	276	76	29	67	34		24	69	26	7	8	126		58	38	833
County Surveyor. N. P. Anderson	276	76	29	67	34		23	69	26	7	8	126		58	36	835
Superintendent District Schools. John D. Peters	276	76	29	67	34		23	69	26	7	8	126		58	38	835

BOX ELDER COUNTY.

PRECINCTS.	For Justices.	No. of Votes. Full Term	No. of Votes. Unex. Term	For Constable.	No. of Votes. Full Term	No. of Votes. Unex. Term
Box Elder........	J. B. McMaster....		258	L. S. Wright.....	260	
" "	Jonah Mathias......	258				
Bear River	M. C. Mortensen.,..	76		Chris Petersen....	76	
Curlew...........	Alex. A. Glen......	29		Jas. Cottam......	29	
Call's Fort	B. H. Talman......	67		Thos. Wheatley, Jr.	67	
Park Valley	Wm. H. Mecham...	32		E. D. Mecham....	33	
" "	Wm. Godfrey......	2				
Kelton...........	No Election.					
Malad	W. A. Thompson...	57		H. H. Smith.....	64	
"	H. House..........	18		W. B. Bradford...	18	
Mantua	L. J. Halling.......	69		C. M. Jensen.....	69	
Grouse Creek.....	E. H. Parsons......	10		F. A. Hales......	26	
" "	Henry Hales.......	7				
" "	B. H. Cook........	10				
Promontory......	No Election.					
Plymouth	E. O. Wilcox	8		G. Wolverton.....	8	
Willard	T. W. Brewerton...	126		J. M. Dalton	126	
Terrace	No Election.					
Portage	Henry John........		56	Jas. Halford......	56	
"	Isaac Allen, Sr.....	56		H. F. Smith	56	
Deweyville.......	D. W. Holdaway...	33		J. C. Dewey.. ..	35	

Fence Viewers—Curlew, Wm. Hudson, 291 votes.

CACHE COUNTY.

COUNTY OFFICERS.	Logan.	Mendon.	Hyrum.	Providence.	Millville.	Peterborough.	Wellsville.	Trenton.	Clarkston.	Paradise.	Richmond.	Lewiston.	Hyde Park.	Newton.	Benson.	Smithfield.	Total.
Judge of Probate, unexpired term. James Z. Stewart.	505	128	173	84	90	10	197	22	61	114	187	131	63	42	25	235	2067
Clerk of the County Court, unexpired term. Willard W. Maughan.	506	128	173	84	90	10	197	24	61	114	187	131	63	42	25	235	2070
One Selectman, unexpired term, one year. P. T. Moorehead.	506	128	173	84	90	10	197	24	61	114	187	131	63	41	25	235	2069
One Selectman, unexpired term, two years. A. A. Allen.	506	128	173	84	90	10	197	24	61	114	187	131	63	42	25	235	2070
Assessor, unexpired term. L. R. Martineau.	505	128	173	84	90	10	197	24	61	114	187	131	63	42	25	235	2069
Collector, unexpired term. L. R. Martineau.	505	128	173	84	90	10	197	24	61	114	187	131	63	42	25	235	2069
County Recorder, unexpired term. Jno. A. McAllister.	501	128	172	84	90	10	197	24	61	114	187	131	63	42	25	235	2064
Coroner, unexpired term. Jno. E. Carlisle.	506	128	173	84	90	10	197	24	61	114	187	131	63	42	25	235	2070
Sheriff. N. W. Crookston.	506	128	173	84	90	10	197	24	61	114	187	131	63	42	25	235	2070
County Prosecuting Attorney, unexpired term. W. W. Maughan.	506	128	173	84	90	10	197	24	61	114	187	131	63	42	25	235	2070
County Surveyor, unexpired term. Edward Hanson.	506	128	173	84	90	10	197	24	61	114	187	131	63	42	25	234	2069
One Selectman. Fred Turner.	506	128	173	84	90	10	197	24	61	114	187	131	63	42	25	235	2070
W. V. Carbine.		128	173	84	90	10	197	24	61	114	187	131	63	18	25	235	2046
Superintendent of District Schools. W. H. Apperly.	506													25			25

CACHE COUNTY.

PRECINCTS.	For Justices.	No. of Votes Full Term	No. of Votes Unex.Term	For Constable.	No. of Votes Full Term	No. of Votes Unex.Term
Logan	B. F. Cummings, Jr.	487		J. W. Quayle	506	
"	M. H. Farnes	505		John Larsen	506	
Mendon	Chris. Sorenson		124	George W. Baker		127
Hyrum	J. J. Hensen	172		Wells McBride		173
Providence	Wm. Smith	84		J. Zollenger		71
Milleville	Jos. Humphries	89		H. S. Hulse		87
Peterborough	Wm. Kidman, Sr.	10		Michael Erikson		10
Wellsviile	Thomas Bradshaw	171		David Murray		171
Trenton	John Bingham	24		John Sandberg		24
Clarkston	H. Stokes		61	John Thompson		61
Paradise	James Lofthouse	114		D. Bickmore		114
Richmond	S. H. Hobson	185		James Johnson		184
Lewiston	Jno. M. Bernhisel	131		W. A. Terry		131
Hyde Park	N. Christensen	63		M. Woolfe		63
Newton	W. H. Griffin	41		J. P. Jensen		42
Benson	Jonathan Ricks	21		Ed. Clark		25
"	Robert Rewnly	4				
Smithfield	Jas. Kirkbride	234		Samuel Nelson		23

DAVIS COUNTY.

COUNTY OFFICERS.	South Weber.	Kaysville.	South Hooper.	Farmington.	Centerville.	Bountiful.	South.	West.	Total.
Judge of Probate, unexpired term.									
David Stoker....................	32	218	52	130	81	145	88	43	789
A. L. Buckland	14	11	12	12	9	14	5		77
Clerk of the County Court, unexpired term.									
Jacob Miller...................	32	218	52	130	81	146	87	44	790
Michael Pilling	14	11	12	12	9	14	5		77
One Selectman, unexpired term, two years.									
Thos. F. Rouesche.............	32	217	52	129	81	146	88	44	789
Henry Southworth	14	11	12	12	9	14	5		77
Assessor and Collector, unexpired term.									
Jas. H. Wilcox.................	32	218	52	131	81	146	88	44	792
H. W. Haight..................	14	11	12	12	9	14	5		77
Sheriff.									
T. F. King.....................	32	218	52	124	81	146	88	44	785
Jesse W. Smith	14	11	12	13	9	14	5		78
County Surveyor, unexpired term.									
Chas. C. Hyde.................	32	218	52	131	81	146	88	44	792
Orson P. Buckland	14	11	12	12	9	14	5		77
Coroner.									
E. F. Rose	32	218	52	131	81		88	44	646
Parley P. Evans...............	14	11	12	12	9		5		63
County Prosecuting Attorney, unexpired term.									
Henry L. Steed................	32	218	52	131	81	146	87	44	791
T. J. Brandon	14	11	12	12	9	14	5		77
One Selectman.									
B. F. Knowlton................	32	217	52	129	81	146	88	44	789
Jno. Bowman....	14	12	12	12	9	14	5		78
County Treasurer, unexpired term.									
E. B. Clark	32	218	52	131	81	146	88	44	792
Adelbert Burnham..............	14	11	12	12	9	14	5		77
Superintendent of District Schools.									
L. H. Kennard.................	32	218	52	131	81	146	88	44	792
David Peebles	14	11	12	12	9	14	5		77

DAVIS COUNTY.

PRECINCTS.	For Justices.	No. of Votes. Full Term	No. of Votes. Unex.Term	For Constable.	No. of Votes. Full Term	No. of Votes. Unex.Term
South Weber	P. P. Prophet	32		Jas. H. Cook	32	
" "	Thomas H. Peck	14		W. A. Bowman	14	
Kaysville	C. C. Hyde	219		Levi Taylor		219
South Hooper	Levi Hammon	53		Heber C. Smith	54	
" "	Joseph Messervy	2				
Farmington	T J. Steed	130		W. V. Haight	131	
"	W. Walker	12		W. Anderson	12	
Centerville	A. B. Porter	81		C. W. Rockwood	81	
"	And. Dalrymple	9		Milton Ward	9	
Bountiful	G. A. Lincoln	146		Chas. H. Rampton	146	
"	Jas. W. Burnham	4		John Poorman	4	
South	R. E. Egan	89		Eric Hogan	87	
West	Lewis M. Grant	44		Thomas Roberts	44	

	For Fence Viewers.	
South Hooper	Joseph Messervy	52
" "	Edwin Parker	52
Farmington	Thomas Abbott	97
"	Thomas Rogers	97
"	L. P. Anderson	12
"	Alfred Wharton	10
Centerville	Richard Mills	9
"	John Duncan	9
South	James Moss	45
"	Joseph Parkin	45

EMERY COUNTY.

COUNTY OFFICERS.	Scofield.	Castle Dale.	Ferron.	Huntington.	Moab.	Price.	Total.
Judge of Probate, unexpired term.							
Orange Seeley	2	78	53	68			201
L. Granger	1						1
Clerk of the County Court, unexpired term.							
J. H. Whitney	2	78	53	68			201
One Selectman, unexpired term, two years.							
J. T. Ballantine	1						1
A. Nielsen		78	53	68			199
Assessor and Collector, unexpired term.							
T. H. Thomas	1						1
J. D. Kilpack		78	52	68			198
Coroner, unexpired term.							
D. W. Holdaway	17	78	53	68			216
Sheriff, unexpired term.							
Wm. Fitzsimmons	1						1
Jno. C. Snow		77		67			144
Hiram Loveless			46				46
County Prosecuting Attorney, unexpired term.							
L. Granger	1						1
John K. Reid		78	53	68			199
County Surveyor, unexpired term.							
Chas. E. Wallace	1						1
Elias H. Cox	1	78	53	68			200
County Treasurer, unexpired term.							
John L. Nelson	1						1
C. G. Larsen, Jr		78	53	68			199
One Selectman.							
A. H. Sturgis	1						1
J. W. Seeley		72	53	68			193
Superintendent of District Schools.							
John Eden	1						1
E. H. Cox		78	53	68			199

PRECINCTS.	For Justices.	No. of Votes.		For Constable.	No. of Votes.	
		Full Term.	Unex. Term		Full Term.	Unex. Term
Scofield	S. J. Harkness	16		R. J. Wright	17	
"	L. Granger	1				
Castle Dale	J. K. Reid		78	A. Tuttle		78
Ferron	Eph. Homer	53		Jos. S. Stevens	53	
Huntington	N. H. Stevens		68	J. E. Johnson		68
Moab	O. W. Warner	16		W. H. Allred	20	
Price						

GARFIELD COUNTY.

COUNTY OFFICERS.	Hillsdale.	Cannonville.	Panguitch.	Clover Flat.	Escalante.	Total.
Judge of Probate.						
David Cameron............................	24	28	102		61	215
Clerk of the County Court.						
Jno. M. Dunning...........................	24	28	105		61	218
One Selectman.						
James Houston............................	24	28	104		61	217
One Selectman, unexpired term, one year.						
Allen Miller...........................	24	28	105		61	218
One Selectman, unexpired term, two years.						
Erastus Beck.............................	24	28	105		58	215
Assessor and Collector.						
Robt. P. Allen............................	24	28	101		61	214
County Prosecuting Attorney.						
Jno. Houston.............................	24	28	105		61	218
Coroner.						
R. C. Pinney.............................	24	28	102		61	215
Sheriff.						
Jos. Marshall............................	24	28	105		61	218
County Treasurer.						
John Meyers.............................			35		20	55
County Recorder.						
Jas. A. Worthen.........................	24	28	105		61	218
County Surveyor.						
Jas. B. Heywood.........................	24	28	105		61	218
Superintendent of District Schools.						
Jas. B. Heywood.........................	24	28	105		61	218

PRECINCTS.	For Justices.	No. of Votes. Full Term.	No. of Votes. Unex. Term.	For Constable.	No. of Votes. Full Term.	No. of Votes. Unex. Term.
Hillsdale.........	Jas. F. Johnson.....	24		L. Van Leuven....	24	
Cannonville.......	W. S. Lewman.....	27		W. A. Thompson.	28	
Panguitch.........	M. W. Foy........	104		J. W. Pace........	105	
"	John E. Myers......		100			
Escalante.........	O. W. Allen.......	60		Jos. S. Barney....	56	

IRON COUNTY.

COUNTY OFFICERS.	Parowan.	Cedar.	Paragoonah.	Kanarrah.	Summit.	Total.
Judge of Probate, unexpired term.						
William C. McGregor	146	129	53	39	20	587
Clerk of the County Court, unexpired term.						
John E. Dalley	149	129	53	39	20	390
One Selectman, unexpired term, one year.						
William Davenport	113	42	20	39	20	234
Myron S. Roundy	35	86	18			139
John Topham			13			13
One Selectman, unexpired term, two years.						
John Parry	149	126	52	39	20	386
Assessor and Collector, unexpired term.						
Chas. Adams	112	43	40	39	20	254
E. Parry	36	86	12			134
County Recorder, unexpired term.						
William H. Holyoak	148	128	53	39	20	388
Coroner, unexpired term.						
F. W. Pendleton	149	129	53	39	20	390
Sheriff, unexpired term.						
Hugh L. Adams	118	128	43	39	20	348
Wm. O. Orton	31		10			41
County Prosecuting Attorney, unexpired term.						
J. W. Brown	107	32	19	37	20	215
Wm. Davenport	42	88	33			163
County Surveyor, unexpired term.						
Mayhew H. Dalley	149	129	53	39	20	390
One Selectman.						
Morgan Richards, Jr	114	42	32	39	20	247
John Topham	37	87	21			145
Superintendent of District Schools.						
M. H. Dalley	149	127	53	39	20	388

PRECINCTS.	For Justices.	No. of Votes. Full Term.	No. of Votes. Unex.Term.	For Constable.	No. of Votes. Full Term.	No. of Votes. Unex.Term.
Parowan	John H. Henderson	146		E. Wardell	149	
Cedar	John Chatterby	126		C. C. Bladen		128
Paragoonah	John R. Robinson	53		D. A. Lamoreaux	49	
Kanarrah	Wm. Ford	39		Wm. K. Williams	39	
Summit	Jas. H. Dalley	20	20	Wm. Smith	20	

	For Fence Viewers.	
Parowan	William Gerr	148
"	William W. Pendleton	148
Cedar	William Tucker	128
"	William D. Lee	127
Paragoonah	John R. Robinson, Jr	52
"	S. T. Topham	51
Summit	S. S. Hulett	20
"	Jos. B. Dalley	20

JUAB COUNTY.

COUNTY OFFICERS.	Nephi.	Mona.	Levan.	Tintic.	Total.
Judge of Probate, unexpired term.					
Charles Foot.................................	13	21	9	41	84
Joel Grover..................................	350	37	65	2	454
Clerk of the County Court, unexpired term.					
Wm. A. C. Bryan............................	361	61	74	41	537
Alma Hague.................................				1	1
One Selectman, unexpired term, one year.					
Eli Curtis...................................	362	61	74	42	539
One Selectman, unexpired term, two years.					
Jos. A. Hyde................................	363	61	74	42	540
Assessor and Collector, unexpired term.					
Wm. A. C. Bryan............................	350	59	69	30	508
Edwin R. Booth.............................	8		5	13	26
Sheriff, unexpired term.					
Samuel Cazier...............................	363	61	74	43	541
Coroner, unexpired term.					
Henry Adams................................	363	61	74	43	541
County Prosecuting Attorney, unexpired term.					
F. W. Chappell..............................	356	45	69	25	495
Jos. Vickers................................	2	16	5	13	36
One Selectman.					
Thos. Wright, Jr............................	363	60	74	42	539
County Surveyor, unexpired term.					
John Foote..................................	363	61	74	43	541
Superintendent of District Schools, unexpired term.					
F. W. Chappell..............................	363	61	74	43	41

PRECINCTS.	For Justices.	No. of Votes Full Term	No. of Votes Unex. Term	For Constable.	No. of Votes Full Term	No. of Votes Unex. Term
Nephi...........	Lyman L. Hudson..	357		John Sidwell.....	349	
Mono...........	Samuel P. Ewing..		33	W. P. Borrowman.		350
"	E. W. Williams....	29		Joel A. Bascomb..		58
Levan...........	A. L. Jackman.....	74		James German....	56	
"	Heber W. Hartley..	74		Chas. Mangelson..	75	
Tintic............	James Shearer......	33		W. J. Durfey.....	19	
"	F. W. Lamb........	11		John Martenson...	23	

	For Fence Viewers.		
Tintic...........	I. J. Howell..	9	
"	J. W. Reid...	9	

KANE COUNTY.

COUNTY OFFICERS.	Glendale.	Orderville.	Mt. Carmel.	Pareah.	Kanab.	Johnson.	Upper Kanab.	Total.
Judge of Probate, unexpired term.								
John S. Carpenter	34				19		14	67
John Rider		26	16		28	10		80
Joel H. Johnson				18				18
Clerk of the County Court, unexpir'd term								
W. D. Johnson					18			18
Joel H. Johnson	34	26	21		47	10	14	152
C. N. Carroll				18				18
One Selectman, unexpired term, two years								
W. D. Johnson		26	21		28	10		85
Taylor Crosby	34				19		14	67
One Selectman, unexpired term, one year.								
B. Y. Beard	34	26	21		47	10		138
Homer A. Bouton				18				18
Assessor and Collector, unexpired term.								
W. H. Roundy	34		13		19		14	80
W. H. Laws		26	6		28	9		69
Z. K. Judd				18				18
Coroner, unexpired term.								
Z. K. Judd, Sr	34	26	21		47		14	142
Wm. A. Carroll				18				18
Coroner, full term.								
Z. K. Judd	34	26	21			10	14	105
Sheriff.								
Haskel Jolly	34	26	21		47	10	14	152
County Prosecuting Attorney, unex. term.								
Willard Carroll	34	26	21		47	10	14	152
John E. Riggs				18				18
County Surveyor, unexpired term.								
Homer A. Bouton	34	26			47	10	14	131
W. H. Laws				18				18
County Treasurer.								
John E. Riggs	34	26	21		47	10	14	152
Haskell Jolly				18				18
Recorder.								
Joel H. Johnson	34	26	21	18	47	10	14	170
County Surveyor.								
Homer A. Bouton	34	26	21				14	95
One Selectman.								
Robert Monceur	28	26	17		19		14	104
C. M. Carroll	6				28	10		45
B. Y. Beard				18			14	32
Superintendent of District Schools.								
Jas. McAllister	34	26	21	18	47	10	14	170

KANE COUNTY.

PRECINCTS.	For Justices.	No. of Votes. Full Term	No. of Votes. Unex.Term	For Constable.	No. of Votes. Full Term	No. of Votes. Unex.Term
Glendale	Silas Harris	34		Silas Brinkerhoff	34	
Orderville	H. A. Fowler		26	Henry Hart		26
Mt. Carmel	David Stevenson	10		Wyatt Bryan	20	
" "	Wm. Jolly	11				
Pareah	Nephi Smithson	18		Thos. Smith	18	
Kanab	W. S. Lewis	47		Adolphus Young		47
Johnson	W. D. Johnson	10		Spencer Shumway	10	
Upper Kanab	W. H. Roundy	14		B. O. Roundy	14	

MILLARD COUNTY.

COUNTY OFFICERS.	Meadow.	Kanosh.	Filmore.	Holden.	Scipio.	Oak Creek.	Lemington.	Deseret.	Total.
Judge of Probate, unexpired term.									
Hyrum Mace	56	95	138	78	92	28	38	97	622
Thos. Turner			2						2
Clerk of the County Court, unexpired term.									
W. H. King	56	95	141	79	92	28	38	97	626
One Selectman, unexpired term, two years.									
David Sephens	56	95	141	79	91	28	38	97	625
Assessor and Collector, unexpired term.									
T. C. Callister	56	95	141	79	92	28	38	97	626
Coroner, unexpired term.									
Jas. McMahon	56	95	140	79	92	28	38	97	625
Sheriff, unexpired term.									
Jos. Holbrook	56	95	141	79	92	28	38	97	626
County Prosecuting Attorney, unexpired term.									
Jos. S. Giles	56	95	141	79	92	28	38	97	626
County Surveyor, unexpired term.									
J. S. Giles	56	95	141	79	92	28	38	97	626
One Selectman.									
George Crane	56	94	141	77	92	28	38	97	623
Superintendent of District Schools.									
T. C. Callister	56	95	141	79	92	28	38	97	626

PRECINCTS.	For Justices.	Full Term.	Unex. Term.	For Constable.	Full Term.	Unex. Term.
Meadow	S. M. Smith		56	David Duncan		56
Kanosh	George Crane		70	John Charlesworth		94
"	C. H. Bennett		20			
Filmore	C. P. Beauregard	141		C. C. Beauregard.	141	
"	W. H. King		141			
Holden	B. J. Stringan		79	Geo. W. Nixon		79
Scipio	H. N. McArthur		91	Peter Quarenberg.		91
Oak Creek	Geo. Finlanson.		28	E. L. Lyman		18
Lemington	C. Overson		34	J. C. Mecham		35
"	L. W. Stout		4	Don C. Walker		3
Deseret	L. R. Cropper	93		J. W. Damron	93	

MORGAN COUNTY.

COUNTY OFFICERS.	Morgan.	Canyon Creek	Milton.	Peterson.	Croyden.	Total.
Judge of Probate, unexpired term.						
J. R. Porter	88	80	19	31	22	240
Jesse Haven	2		23	1	18	44
Clerk of the County Court, unexpired term.						
S. Francis	91	80	24	35	41	271
Jas. Durant			24			24
One Selectman, unexpired term, one year.						
W. H. Toone	92	81	50	35	21	279
Gibson Condie					20	20
One Selectman, unexpired term, two years.						
I. C. Gaarder	92	81	50	35	41	299
Assessor and Collector, unexpired term.						
Henry Eddington	78	64	20	27	18	207
F. Kingston	21	22	30	7	23	103
Sheriff.						
John H. Dickson	93	81	50	35	41	300
County Recorder.						
Samuel Francis	92	80	31	35	41	279
T. R. G. Welch			10			10
Coroner.						
Andrew Poulson	92	81	50	35	41	299
County Prosecuting Attorney, unexpired term.						
Jas. R. Stewart	92	81	50	35	40	298
One Selectman.						
John H. Rich	89	81	50	35	41	296
George Hiner	3					3
County Surveyor, unexpired term.						
E. W. Hunter	93	81	50	35	41	300
Superintendent of District Schools.						
Jas. E. Stephenson	90	81	49	35	39	294

PRECINCTS.	For Justices.	No. of Votes. Full Term.	No. of Votes. Unex. Term.	For Constable.	No. of Votes. Full Term.	No. of Votes. Unex. Term.
Morgan	Jas. Durant	92		Henry Eddington		93
Canyon Creek	Oscar O. Stoddard		66	Jos. Waldron		66
Milton	George Cuddle	39		Martin Caarder	40	
Peterson	Ole O. Wold	23		A. B. Anderson	22	
"	John Green	9		Silas H. Card	10	
Croyden	George Thackery	22		Chas. J. Toone	21	
"	W. H. Toone	14		Geo. W. Chapman	14	

	For Fence Viewers.		
Canyon Creek	John H. Rich		66
"	Alma Porter		66

PIUTE COUNTY.

COUNTY OFFICERS.	Thurber.	Circleville.	Fremont.	Greenville.	Wilmont.	Bullion.	Deer Trail.	Total.
Judge of Probate, unexpired term.								
Rufus A. Allan	67	30	74	45		4		220
Jos. Whittaker		25	4		5	21	5	60
Clerk of the County Court, unexp'd term.								
Cnrtis E. Bolton	67	33	74	45	4	1	1	225
Chas. Morrill		24	4		5	21	5	59
One Selectman, unexpired term, two years								
Volney King	67	30	73	45	4	4		223
Hugh J. McLellan		23	11		5	21	5	65
Assessor and Collector, unexpired term.								
Jas. W. Bay	67	28	74	45	4	4		222
John S. Balch		23	4		5	21	6	59
Coroner, unexpired term.								
Horatio Morrill	67	33	73	45	4	4		226
James Wyley		7	4			19	5	35
Sheriff, unexpired term.								
D. S. Gillis	67	30	73	45	4	4		223
John S. Baler		24	4		5	20	6	59
County Prosecuting Attorney, unexp'd term								
David Rufus Taylor	67	34	74	45	4	4		228
Miles Durkee		23	4		5	17	6	55
County Surveyor.								
Thos. E. King	67	33	73	45	4	3	1	226
Samuel J. McCormick		22	4		5	20	5	56
One Seleetman.								
George Brinkerhof	67	34	68	45	4	4		222
Frank C. Murry		24	4			21	5	54
Superintendent of District Schools.								
Leonard G. Long	67	35	45	45	4	4		228
W. L. Jones		23	4		5	20	6	59

PRECINCTS.	For Justices.	No. of Votes. Full Term	No. of Votes. Unex.Term	For Constable.	No. of Votes. Full Term	No. of Votes. Unex.Term
Thurber	Jas. W. Hunt	67		Wm. Meeks	67	
Circleville	Jas. Wylie		32	D. S. Willis		26
"	Jas. Lewis		20	Chas. Dalton		21
Fremont	John T. Lazenby	67		Wm. Turner	74	
"	J. Goff	7				
Greenville	Leonard G. Long		45	O. M. Manville		45
Wilson	Andrew Grick	5		J. J. Riddle		5
"	J. D. Wilcox	4		J. Nichols		4
Bullion	Dewitt C. Tate		24	John Lee	15	
"	Frank C. Murry	25		Philip Gauchett	5	
Deer Trail	F. C. Murry	6		Philip Gauchett	5	
" "	Dewitt C. Tate	5		Harry Wilson	1	

RICH COUNTY.

COUNTY OFFICERS.	Woodruff.	Randolph.	Laketown.	Meadowville.	Garden City.	Total.
Judge of Probate, unexpired term.						
W. R. Walton....................................	43	55	41	11	41	191
Clerk of the County Court, unexpired term.						
Wm. Rex...	43	54	41	10	41	189
One Selectman, unexpired term, two years.						
Robert Calder	43	55	41	11	41	191
Assessor and Collector, unexpired term.						
Jos. U. Eldredge.............................	40	50	15	9	41	155
Alma Findley..................................			27			27
Coroner, unexpired term.						
John S. Jones.................................	43	55	41	11	41	191
Sheriff, unexpired term.						
Anson C. Call.................................	43	55	41	11	41	191
County Prosecuting Attornoy, unexpired term.						
E. Lee...	39	54	40	11		144
R. S. Spence...................................					41	41
County Surveyor, unexpired term.						
Joshua Eldredge..............................	41	55	40	11	41	188
One Selectman.						
Joseph Kimball................................	43	55	41	9	41	189
Superintendent of District Schools.						
R. S. Spence	43	55	42	10	41	191

PRECINCTS.	For Justices.	No. of Votes. Full Term.	No. of Votes. Unex. Term.	For Constable.	No. of Votes. Full Term.	No. of Votes. Unex. Term.
Woodruff........	N. C. Vorse.......	41		E. Lee.............	40	
Randolph	Jno. Snowball......		50	O. Jacobson........		50
Laketown	A. Findley.........		41	Geo. Early, Jr....		41
Meadowville......	Geo. Judd	11		Josh Eldredge		11
Garden City......	D. S. Cook		41	Geo. Whitington..		41

	For Fence Viewers.	
Woodruff.........	Chas. Dean....................................	43
"	A. E. Eastman................................	43
Randolph	Jno. Kennedy.................................	55
"	Chas. South....................................	55
Laketown	E. G. Lamborn................................	42
"	Geo. Early, Jr.,................................	42
Meadowville......	Aaron Nebeker................................	11
"	Josh Eldredge.................................	11
Garden City......	W. A. Moore...................................	41
"	Jos. W. Cook..................................	39

SAN JUAN COUNTY.

COUNTY OFFICERS.	Bluff.	Montezuma.	Total.
Judge of Probate, unexpired term.			
John Allen, Jr.	50	7	57
Clerk of the County Court, unexpired term.			
Chas. E. Walton.	50	7	57
One Selectman, unexpired term, two years.			
Henry H. Herriman.	50	7	57
Assessor and Collector, unexpired term.			
Samuel H. Redd.	49	7	56
Coroner, unexpired term.			
John Pace.	49	7	56
Sheriff, unexpired term.			
Amasa M. Barton.	49	7	56
County Prosecuting Attorney, unexpired term.			
Jas. B. Decker.	50	7	57
County Surveyor, unexpired term.			
Peter Allen.	50	7	57
County Treasurer, unexpired term.			
Samuel Wood.	46	7	53
One Selectman.			
Wm. Robb.	49	7	56
Superintendent of District Schools.			
Jos. A. Lyman.	49	7	56

PRECINCTS.	For Justices.	No. of Votes.		For Constable.	No. of Votes.	
		Full Term.	Unex.Term.		Full Term.	Unex.Term.
Bluff City	John F. Barton	49		J. E. Eyre	49	
Montezuma	Henry Holyoak		7	Caleb Tait		7

SALT LAKE COUNTY.

COUNTY OFFICERS.	1st Salt Lake.	2nd Salt Lake.	3d Salt Lake.	4th Salt Lake.	5th Salt Lake.	Farmers.	Ft. Herriman.	Butler.	East Mill Creek	Union.	Granite.	West Jordan.	Big Cottonw'd.	Granger.	Mountain Dell.	South Jordan.	Hunter.	Silver.	So. Cottonw'd.	L'tle Cottonw'd	North Point.	Bingham.	Riverton.	Pleasant Green	Brighton.	North Jordan.	Sugar House.	Draper.	Mill Creek.	Sandy.	Totals.
Judge of Probate, unexpired term. Elias A. Smith	167	629	390		400	45 2	48 16	29 2	67 2	63 8	25 1	160 1	107 4	37 2	13	48	19	5 0	151 9	26	20	98 1	44	51	30 6	79 1	87 9	132 3	196 3	99 1:	4061 341
E. D. Hoge	36	30	17		42	46 2	48 16	29 2	67 2	67 2	25 1	160 1	107 4	37 2	13	48	19	5	151 9	26	20	98 1	44	52	30 6	80 1	87 9	133 1	196 •	99 10	4083 332
Clerk of the County Court, unex. term. John O. Cutter	470 35	646 28	614 10	391 17	403 43	46 2	48 16	29 2	67 3	67 2	25 1	160 1	107 4	37 2	13	48	19	5 9	150 9	26	20	98 1	44	52	30 6	80	87 9	133 3	196 3	99 10	4081 331
J. F. Bradley																															
One Selectman, unex. term, two years. E. M. Weller	471 33	644 29	614 10	391 17	402 43	46 2	48 16	29 2	67 2	67 2	25 1	160 1	107 4	37 2	13	48	19	5 9	151 9	26	20	98 1	44	52	30 6	80	87 9	133 3	196 3	99 10	4081 316
J. D. Lomax																															
Assessor, unexpired term. W. S. Burton	469 35	644 29	612 10	399 16	403 43	46 2	48 15	29 2	67 2	67 2	25 1	160 1	107 4	37 2	13	48	19	5	151 9	26	20	98 1	45	51	30 6	80	87 9	133 3	196 3	99 10	4078 333
Collector, unexpired term. Arthur Pratt	464 35	639 12	603 10	382 17	385 43	45 2	48 16	29 2	67 2	67 3	25 1	160 1	107 4	37 2	13	49	19	5	151 9	27	20	98 1	45	52	3 6 1	76 1	87 9	133 3	196 3	99 10	4032 317
N. V. Jones																															
Sheriff, unexpired term. Ed. L. Butterfield	470 35	646 29	614 10	391 17	403 43	46 2	48 16	29 2	67 2	67 2	25 1	160 1	107 4	37 2	13	48	19	5	151 9	26	20	98 1	44	51	30 6	80	87 9	133 3	196 3	99 10	4075 315
John A. Groesbeck																															
County Surveyor, unexpired term. J. W. Greenman	470 35	646 29	614 10	391 17	403 43	46 2	48 16	29 2	67 2	66 2	25 1	150 1	107 4	37 2	13	48	19	5	151 9	26	20	98 1	44	52	29 6	80	87 9	133 1	196 3	99 10	4081 316
J. D. H. McAllister																															
Coroner, unexpired term. T. C. Bailey	470 35	646 12	614 10	391 17	403 43	46 2	48 16	29 2	67 2	67 2	25 1	160 1	107 4	37 2	13	48	19	5	151 9	26	20	98 1	44	52	29 6	80	87 9	133 1	196 3	99 10	4081 316
George J. Taylor																															
County Prosecut'g Attorney, unex. term John F. Hardie	470 35	614 29	614 10	399 7	403 42	46 2	48 16	29 2	67 2	67 2	25 1	160 1	107 4	37 2	13	48	19	5	151 9	26	20	98 1	44	51	30 6	80	87 9	133 1	196 3	99 10	4081 331
Isaac M. Waddell																															
Selectman full term. Edward P. Sutherland	479 35	611 29	614 10	391 17	402 43	46 2	48 16	29 2	67 2	67 2	25 1	160 1	107 4	37 2	13	48	19	5	151 9	26	20	98 1	44	52	29 6	80	87 9	133 3	196 3	99 10	4074 333
Ezekiel Holman																															
County Treasurer. Samuel Kahn	470 35	615 29	613 10	390 17	403 43	46 2	48 16	29 2	67 2	65 2	25 1	160 1	107 4	37 2	13	48	19	5	151 9	26	20	98 1	44	51	30 6	80	87 9	133 1	196 3	99 10	4731 315
M. E. Cummings																															
W. S. McCormick	35	29	10	17	42	46 2	48 16	29 2	67 2	67 2	25 1	160 1	107 4	37 2	13	48	19	5 9	151 9	26	20	98 1	44	52	30 6	80	87 9	133 1	196 3	99 10	1082 332
Superintendent of District Schools. John Morgan	470 1	615	614	391	403	46	48	29	67	67	25	139	107	37	13	48	19		151	26	20	98	44	52	30	80	87	133	196	99	4081 1
Orson Howard																															

SALT LAKE COUNTY.

PRECINCTS.	For Justices.	No. of Votes. Full Term.	No. of Votes. Unex.Term.	For Constable.	No. of Votes. Full Term.	No. of Votes. Unex.Term.
1st, Salt Lake	Adam Speirs	470		James Malin	469	
"	C. H. M. y'Agramonte		36			
2nd, Salt Lake	N. F. Cowly	646		R. F. Turnbow	646	
3rd, Salt Lake	Wm. C. Neal	614		Henry Arnold, Jr	614	
4th, Salt Lake	Jos. F. Simmons	391		Jos. Burt	391	
5th, Salt Lake	Geo. D. Pyper	403		Chas H. Crow	393	
Farmers	Alma Pratt	46		B. L. Adams	46	
Fort Harriman	Henry Crane	48		John M. Bowen	48	
Butler	Wm. McGhite	30		S. S. Jones	20	
East Mill Creek	John Osgathorpe		69	Jos. E. Morris	69	
Union	Willard C. Bergen		68	Jno. H. Walker		50
"				Thos. Smith		19
Granite	Theo. Powell	8		Geo. Thomson	8	
"	Wm Thompson, Jr	17		David Despain	17	
West Jordan	Benj. L. Cutler		160	D. R. Bateman	160	
Big Cottonwood	Francis McDonald		107	L. A. Howard	107	
Granger	Daniel McRae		15	John McKay	39	
"	M. D. Cook		15			
"	Ross Porter		7			
Mountain Dell	Bines Dixon		13	Richard Winmill	13	
South Jordan	John Holt	48		Geo. S. Beckstead	48	
Hunter	Jos. N. Morris		19	Alfred A. Jones	19	
South Cottonwood	Orson A. Woolly		156	Wm. Royce, Jr	148	
"				Wm. Jamison	7	
Little Cottonwood	J. C. Morrill	17		John Stilwell	25	
"	E. B. Jones	22		Patrick Snovel	24	
"	W. B. Jones	8				
North Point	Wm. Langford	20		Jos. Hanson	20	
Bingham	John Brunton		59	Jos. Johannigmeir	23	
"	L. B. Kirney		46	P. C. Rooney	23	
Riverton	J. G. Wilder		42	J. De Witt	3	
"	Chas. E. Miller		41	Robert Dansie	44	
Pleasant Grove	Edward Lanbert	52		Austin M. Brown	52	
Brighton	A. G. Adamson	30		Jno. R. Jones	30	
"	O. J. Rogers	5				
North Jordan	Samuel Bringhurst	80		Jos. Lindsey	80	
Sugar House	L. S. Clark	87		O. S. Hardy	87	
Draper	John Fitzgerald		132	Jos. Terry	132	
Mill Creek	E. F. N Guest		196	Jos. R. Carlisle	196	
Sandy	Isaac Harrison		103	Neils Nelson	97	

SAN PETE COUNTY.

COUNTY OFFICERS.	Mt. Pleasant.	Spring City.	Ephraim.	Manti.	Petty.	Fayette.	Gunnison.	Chester.	Wales.	Moroni.	Fount'n Green	Fairview.	Thistle.	Winter Qrs.	Mayfield.	Total.
Judge of Probate, unexpired term. Wm. Anderson	188	152	211	220	37	41	99	32	55	136	127	152	11	28	59	1548
Clerk of the County Court, unexpired term. John Reid	189	152	212	221	37	41	98	32	55	136	127	152	11	28	59	1551
One Selectman, unexpired term, two years. John Carter	189	154	212	221	37	42	99	32	55	136	127	152	11	28	59	1553
Assessor, unexpired term. A. F. Merriam	189	154	212	221	37	42	99	32	55	136	127	152	11	28	59	1554
County Recorder, unexpired term. John Reid	189	152	212	221	37	42	99	32	55	135	127	152	11	28	59	1552
Sheriff. Jens P. Larsen	189	154	212	218	36	42	99	32	55	136	127	152	11	28	59	1549
Coroner. John Anderson	189	154	212	221	37	42	99	32	55	136	127	152	11	28	59	1554
County Prosecuting Attorney, unexpired term. Wm. K. Reid	189	150	211	221	37	42	99	32	55	136	127	152	11	28	59	1549
One Selectman. Parlan McFarlan	189	154	212	221	37	42	99	32	55	136	127	152	11	28	59	1554
County Surveyor. John H. Hongard	189	154	212	221	37	42	99	32	55	136	127	152	11	28	59	1554
Superintendent of District Schools. Wm. K. Reid	189	152	212	221	37	42	99	32	55	136	127	152	11	28	59	1552

SAN PETE COUNTY.

PRECINCTS.	For Justices.	No. of Votes. Full Term.	No. of Votes. Unex.Term.	For Constable.	No. of Votes. Full Term.	No. of Votes. Unex.Term.
Mt. Pleasant	Loritz Larsen	188		John Seely	189	
Spring City	Jno. R. Baxter	154		Peter Burrowson		129
"	L. Burdick	4		Jas. Rasmussen		22
Ephraim	J. P. Christensen	202		N. O. Anderson	202	
Manti	J. H. Lowry	221		Jno. Lowry, Jr	221	
Petty	Abner Lowry, Sr	37		Abner Lowry, Jr	37	
Mayfield	Niels C. Anderson		59	Sam'l L. Williams		59
Fayette	Edward Reid	40		Christopher Olston	40	
Gunnison	Jas. Metcalf		99	Lorenzo H. Childs		99
Chester	W. D. Candlan	32		Reddick Allred	32	
Wales	Henry D. Rees	55		Caanan Lewis	55	
Moroni	J. M. Christensen		90	H. M. Bradley		134
"	H. A. Larter		44			
Fountain Green	Amos P. Johnson		127	Winfield S. Miller		127
Fairview	R. W. Westwood		152	Christian Peterson		152
Thistle	M. V. Sellman	11		Hyrum Seely	11	
Winter Quarters	David J. Williams	28		Jas. Gillespie	21	
"				Robt. McKechney	7	

SEVIER COUNTY.

COUNTY OFFICERS.	Annabella.	Aurora.	Burville.	Central.	Elsinore.	Clenwood.	Joseph.	Salina.	Gooseberry.	Monroe.	Richfield.	Redmond.	Vermillion.	Total.
Judge of Probate, unexpired term.														
Andrew Hepper	24	43	30	33	57	74	59	65	19	83	110	41	18	656
Jas. M. Peterson	2				3	4	6	6	2	32	21		1	77
Clerk of the County Court, unex. term.														
John A. Hellstrom	24	43	30	33	60	78	59	65	19	83	118	41	18	671
One Selectman, unex. term, two years.														
B. H. Greenwood	24	43	30	33	58	74	59	65	19	83	117	41	18	664
August Neilson	2				2	4	6	6	2	32	13		1	68
Assessor and Collector, unexpired term.														
W. H. Clark	24	43	30	33	58	74	59	66	19	82	110	39	18	655
Albert D. Thurber	2				2	4	6	3	2	32	19		1	71
County Recorder, unexpired term.														
John A. Hellstrom	26	43	30	33	60	78	65	71	21	115	131	41	19	733
Sheriff, unexpired term.														
W. H. Clark	24	43	30	33	58	74	59	66	19	83	115	41	18	663
S. F. Mount	2				2	4	6	3	2	32	14		1	66
County Treasurer, unexpired term.														
Hans P. Hansen	24	43	30	33	58	74	59	65	19	83	120	41	18	667
Neils Anderson	2				2	4	6	6	2	32	11		1	66
Coroner, unexpired term.														
Francis A. Perkins	24	43	30	33	58	74	59	64	19	83	116	41	18	662
George Oglevie	2				2	4	6	7	2	32	15		1	71
County Prosecut'g Attorney, unex. term.														
George T. Bean	24	43	30	33	58	74	59	58	19	83	116	41	18	656
E. P. Marquardson	2				2	4	6	5	2	32	15		1	69
D. G. Brown							7							7
One Selectman.														
Albert D. Thurber	24	43	30	33	58	74	59	65	19	83	115	41	18	662
Walter Jones	2				2	4	6	6	2	32	13		1	68
County Surveyor, unexpired term.														
J. M. Petersen	26	43	30	33	60	78	65	71	21	115	131	41	19	733
Superintendent of District Schools.														
Daniel Harrington	24	43	30	33	58	75	59	65	19	84	116	41	18	665
P. D. Stoops					2	3	6	6	2	31	15		1	67

SEVIER COUNTY.

PRECINCTS.	For Justices.	No. of Votes. Full Term	No. of Votes. Unex.Term	For Constable.	No. of Votes. Full Term	No. of Votes. Unex.Term
Annabella	John E. Davis		26	Jos. W. Fairbanks.		26
Aurora	Jos. Kennedy	43		Edward E. Curtis.	43	
Burrville	Myron L. Burr		30	Geo. B. Rust		30
Central	Oscar Rose	32		John H. Avery	33	
Elsinore	Thos. Bell		57	L. Soderberg		58
Glenwood	E. Payne		74	B. Wilson		74
Joseph	Edward Newby		65	W. E. Hyatt		65
Salina	T. G. Humphrey		64	Nathan E. Lewis		64
"	F. G. Willis		5	J. F. Martin		5
Gooseberry	John T. Leonard		19	Jesse E. Billingsly.		19
Monroe	W. A. Warnock	83		Zenos Winget	83	
"	Walter Jones	32		Richard G. Rose	32	
Richfield	Simon Christensen		116	Benjamin Carter		118
Redmond	Chas. Rynerson	41		A. C. Anderson	41	
Vermillion	Peter Gottfredson		18	W. Bells		18

THE TERRITORY OF UTAH.

SUMMIT COUNTY.

COUNTY OFFICERS.	Coalville.	Eche.	Henneferville.	Hoytsville.	Kamas.	Park City.	Peoa.	Rockport.	Snyderville.	Wanship.	Upton.	Total.
Judge of Probate, unexpired term.												
Alma Eldredge	251	28	65	79	131	38	78	27	30	62	39	828
Wm. M. Ferr	22	21	3	1	3	627	5	6	4	13		705
Clerk of the County Court, unexpired term.												
Thos. Alston	246	28	65	79	130	37	80	30	29	58	36	818
Wm. H. Smith	27	18	3	1	3	639	3	2	5	18	3	722
One Selectman, unexpired term, one year.												
John Paskett	250	27	64	78	130	37	80	27	29	63	39	824
Erasmus Sorensen	23	21	3	1	5	641	3	6	6	13		722
One Selectman, unexpired term, two years.												
John Pack, Jr	246	28	59	78	131	36	80	30	28	63	38	817
Ed. C. Morse	27	21	3	3	2	644	3	3	5	13	1	725
Assessor and Collector, unexpired term.												
A. L. Smith	245	31	65	78	132	109	79	28	29	69	38	903
Jas. Ferguson	27	18	3	1	3	526	4	5	5	7	1	600
Coroner, unexpired term.												
Jas. McCormick	251	28	65	78	131	9	79	28	29	54		752
Edwin C. Williamson	22	21	3	1	3	629	4	5	2	12	1	703
Sheriff, unexpired term.												
E. M. Allison	258	34	65	78	133	159	80	30	29	67	39	972
Richard Grant	15	14	3	2	2	505	3	3	6	9		562
County Prosecuting Attorney.												
O. F. Lyons	245	28	65	78	130	41	78	26	23	54	38	806
Wilson T. Snyder	28	21	2	2	3	606	4	7	9	19	1	702
County Surveyor.												
Robt. R. Salmon	250	28	65	79	130	40	79	27	29	59	39	825
Jos. Gorlinski	23	21	3	1	3	613	4	6	5	11		690
County Treasurer, unexpired term.												
Thos. Ball, Sen	251	28	65	79	131	42	80	28	29	63	39	835
Thos. Cupit	22	21	3	1	3	617	3	5	5	13		693
One Selectman.												
Edwin Kimball	273	49	67	88	135	675	83	33	33	70	39	1537
Superintendent of District Schools.												
E. H. Rhead	248	29	64	79	132	34	80	28	29	62	39	824
Jas. H. Kyle	5	2	4	11	3	647	31	5	5	13		726

SUMMIT COUNTY.

PRECINCTS.	For Justices.	No. of Votes. Full Term.	No. of Votes. Unex. Term.	For Constable.	No. of Votes. Full Term.	No. of Votes. Unex. Term.
Coalville	Thos. L. Allan	251		T. L. Beach	251	
"	Thos. Ball		251	A. C. Salmon		241
Echo	Jas. E. Bromley	35		Len. Phillips	43	
Henneferville	R. A. Jones	65		Thos. F. Deering	65	
Hoytsville	Leroy Holt	78		Freeman Malin	78	
Kamas	Geo. C. Pack	131		W. F. Leonard	130	
"	John Vance	131		John Benson	129	
Park City	Wm. Mahoney	499		Terry Brogan		421
"	Thos. Cupit	287		J. R. Lane		246
"	Jos. M. Cohen	357		A. N. Randolph		299
"	Wm. P. Baker	25		Thos. Smith		135
"				J. Cornelius		84
Peoa	John Maxwell	79		Arthur Maxwell		79
Rockport	John M. Malin	31		Thos. Gibbons	32	
Snyderville	Wm. Archibald	26		Jesse Chapman	35	
"	A. W. Beach	9				
Wanship	Geo. Robinson, Sr.	55		J. L. Frazier	65	
"	E. R. Young	6		E. R. Young, Jr.		65
"	C. S. Carter	46				
"	W. Crook	21				
Upton	L. L. Randel	39		John S. Saxton	34	
"				Roland Clark	5	

	For Fence Viewers.	
Coalville	John Wild	251
"	Thos. Beard	251
Echo	Ed. Richins	18
"	Richard Wickell	21
Henneferville	Stephen Beard	65
"	George Jedd	65
Hoytsville	Nephi Sargent	78
"	George Brown	78
Kamas	C. N. Woodard	121
"	John Turnbow	121
Park	J. W. Means	627
"	Peter B. Morris	639
Peoa	A. G. H. Marchan	79
"	J. W. Neal	79
Rockport	A. Vickery	30
"	H. Seamons	30
Snyderville	C. M. Snyder	30
"	D. A. Gibson	15
"	A. W. Beach	20
Wanship	George Carter	61
"	Dan. Bates	63
Upton	Edward Powell	39
"	James Judd	39

TOOELE COUNTY.

COUNTY OFFICERS.	Vernon.	Clover.	Grantsville.	Lake View.	Ophir.	Batesville.	Tooele.	Stockton.	Mill.	Quincy.	Deep Creek.	Total.
Judge of Probate, unexpired term.												
Wm. C. Rydalch............	68	164	28		1	20	175	14	23			493
A. G. Johnson...........		1	1									2
Clerk of the County Court, unexpired term.												
John W. Tate.............	69	170	28		1	20	175	14	24			501
A. J. McChristian.............							8					8
One Selectman, unexpired term, two years.												
Edward J. Arthur............	67	168	28		1	20	183	14	24			505
Peter Hassell.................			2									2
Assessor and Collector, unexpired term.												
A. G. Johnson.............	69	169	28		1	20	183	14	24			508
County Recorder, unexpired term.												
John W. Tate.............	69	170	28	No Returns.	1	20	174	14	24	No Returns.	No Returns.	500
A. J. McChristian.............							7					7
Sheriff, unexpired term.												
Chas. R. McBride............	69	169	28		1	20	171	14	24			496
County Treasurer, unexpired term.												
Thomas Atkins................	69	169	28		1	20	183	14	24			508
Coroner, unexpired term.												
Chas. R. McBride............	69	170	28		1	20	174	14	24			500
County Prosecuting Attorney, unexpired term.												
Thos. W. Lee...............	69	166	28		1	20	172	14	23			495
One Selectman.												
Geo. W. Bryan.............	69	169	28		1	20	181	14	24			506
County Surveyor.												
Alonzo J. Stookey............	67	168	28		1	20	183	14	24			505
Superintendent of District Schools.												
Joshua R. Clark..............	69	171	28		1	20	183	14	24			510

PRECINCTS.	For Justices.	No. of Votes. Full Term	No. of Votes. Elect. Term	For Constable.	No. of Votes. Full Term	No. of Votes. Elect. Term
Clover...........	Isaac J. Caldwell...		35	Alonzo J. Stookey.		69
"	Edward J. Arthur...		34			
Grantsville.......	Wm. H. Green.....	168		O. E. Barnes......	169	
Lake View.....	John B. Smith......		28	Walter Adamson..		28
Ophir...........	H. C. Barstow.....		8	Wm. Robertson...		30
"	Chas. M. Wyman...		27			
Batesville........	John Hillstead......	20		Jas M. Gallagher..	20	
Tooele...........	Alexander Herron...	183		Peter Clegg.......	182	
Stockton.........	R. G. Legg.........	11		J. C. Reynolds....	5	
"	J. C. Reynolds.....	7		Jas. R. Earl......	18	
"	Jas. R. Earl........	13				
Mill.............	F. D. Jacobs........	24		David Powell.....	24	

UINTAH COUNTY.

COUNTY OFFICERS.	Ashley.	Brown's Park.	Total.
Judge of Probate, unexpired term.			
Thos. Bingham..	124		124
Clerk of the County Court, unexpired term.			
Geo. Gemis..,............	123		123
One Selectman, unexpired term, one year.			
M. M. Hall...	88		88
One Selectman, unexpired term, two years.			
L. Johnson..'..........	120		120
Assessor, unexpired term.			
Wm. Ashton....	114		114
Coroner, unexpired term.			
Robt. Bodily..	120		120
Sheriff, unexpired term.			
S. D. Colton..,............	122		122
County Prosecuting Attorney, unexpired term.			
W. P. Reynolds ...'...............................	114		114
One Selectman.			
Jas. Hacking...	120		120
County Treasurer, unexpired term.			
A. S. Johnson	123		123
County Surveyor, unexpired term.			
S. P. Dillman..	119		119
Superintendent of District Schools.			
Jos. H. Black...	119		119

PRECINCTS.	For Justices.	No. of Votes.		For Constable.	No. of Votes.	
		Full Term.	Unex.Term.		Full Term.	Unex.Term.
Ashley	A. S. Johnson......	122		Jas. Hardy........	123	
Brown's Park	A. G. Hadlock.....	115		J. R. Workman...	119	

THE TERRITORY OF UTAH.

UTAH COUNTY.

COUNTY OFFICERS.	Alpine.	American Fork.	Benjamin.	Cedar Fort.	Fairfield.	Goshen.	Lehi.	Provo.	Payson.	Pleasant Grove.	Spanish Fork.	Santaquin.	Spring Lake.	Salem.	Thistle.	Springville.	Total.
Judge of Probate, unexpired term. Warren N. Dusenberry	98	132	27	43	15	72	170	440	304	145	344	127	16	98	17	312	2350
Clerk of the County Court, unexpired term. V. L. Halliday	98	132	27	43	15	72	170	439	304	145	344	127	16	98	17	312	2359
Selectman, unexpired term. Amos D. Holdaway	98	132	27	43	15	72	170	440	304	145	344	127	16	98	17	312	2360
Assessor, unexpired term. Abraham O. Smoot, Jr.	98	131	27	43	15	72	170	439	304	145	344	127	16	98	17	312	2358
Collector, unexpired term. Abraham O. Smoot, Jr.	95	131	27	43	15	72	170	439	304	145	344	127	16	98	17	311	2354
County Recorder, unexpired term. Jos. B. Keeler	98	132	27	43	15	72	170	438	304	145	344	127	16	98	17	312	2358
Sheriff, unexpired term. John W. Turner	98	132	27	43	15	72	170	439	304	145	344	127	16	98	17	312	2360
County Treasurer, unexpired term. Jos. B. Keeler	98	132	27	43	15	72	170	437	304	145	344	127	16	98	17	312	2359
County Prosecuting Attorney, unexpired term. Sam'l R. Thurman	98	132	27	43	15	72	170	440	304	145	344	127	16	98	17	312	2357
Selectman, full term. Jonathan S. Page	98	132	27	43	15	72	170	440	304	145	341	127	16	98	17	311	2356
County Surveyor. Thos. Davies	98	132	27	43	15	72	170	440	304	145	344	127	16	98	17	312	2360
Coroner. John R. Twelves	98	132	27	43	15	72	170	440	304	145	344	127	16	98	17	312	2356
Superintendent of District Schools. Geo. H. Brimhall	98	132	27	43	15	72	170	440	304	145	344	127	16	98	17	312	2360

UTAH COUNTY.

PRECINCTS.	For Justices.	No. of Votes. Full Term	No. of Votes. Unex. Term	For Constable.	No. of Votes. Full Term	No. of Votes. Unex. Term
Alpine	Rich'd T. Booth	63		Henry Noyle	63	
"	Ephraim Healy	39		John Moyle	38	
American Fork	Wm. W. Hunter	134		Jedediah Mercer	131	
Benjamin	Luther K. Stewart		27	Franklyn R. Bills		27
Cedar Fort	L. B. Rhodeback		43	Jas. Rhodeback		43
Fairfield	Wm. H. Carson, Jr.		15	Jas. F. Park		15
Goshen	Eleazer Edwards	57		W. H. Page	52	
"	W. H. Page	15		Robt. Gurley	19	
Lehi	Geo. Webb		170	Thos. Fowler		170
Provo	Jacob F. Gates	438		Wm. Strong		439
"	Wm. H. Brown	439		Jas. H. Clinger		439
Payson	Henry W. Barnett	304		John C. Harper	304	
Pleasant Grove	Jas. O. Bullock	145		Jos. C. Thorne		145
Spanish Fork	Geo. G. Hales		340	Willard O. Creer		344
Santaquin	Thos. B. Heelis	125		Andrew Wallwork	127	
Spring Lake	Albert B. Thomas	16		E. E. Ellsworth	13	
Salem	Andreas Engberg	99		Augustus Bingham	99	
Thistle	S. M. Hicks	9		John T. Moore		17
"	G. A. Hicks		7			
Springville	Abram Noe		287	Oscar M. Moore		289
"	John S. Boyer		21	Aaron Johnson		18

WASHINGTON COUNTY.

COUNTY OFFICERS.	Silver Reef.	Leeds.	Washington.	St. George.	Price.	Santa Clara.	Gunlock.	Hebron.	Pine Valley.	Pinto.	New Harmony.	Virgin City.	Toquerville.	Rockville.	Duncan's Retreat.	Grafton.	Springdale.	Shonesburgh.	Total.
Judge of Probate, unexpired term. Edwin G. Woolley	23	17	78	179	17	33	12	17	59	37	17	57	53	46	12	23	19	11	710
Clerk of the County Court, unexpired term. Jos. C. Bently	23	17	78	179	17	33	12	17	59	37	17	57	53	46	12	23	19	11	711
One Selectman, unexpired term, one year. Richard H. Ashby	23	18	78	179	17	33	12	17	59	37	17	57	53	46	12	23	19	11	710
One Selectman, unexpired term, two years. Jas. P. Terry	23	17	77	179	17	33	12	17	59	37	17	57	53	46	12	23	19	11	709
Assessor and Collector, unexpired term. Augustus P. Hardy	23	17	77	176	17	33	12	17	59	37	17	57	53	46	12	23	19	11	706
County Recorder, unexpired term. Moroni Snow	23	17	78	179	17	33	12	17	59	37	17	57	53	46	12	23	19	11	710
Coroner, unexpired term. Richard Bentley	23	17	78	179	17	33	12	17	59	37	17	57	53	46	12	23	19	11	710
Sheriff, unexpired term. Augustus P. Hardy	23	17	78	178	17	33	12	17	59	37	17	57	53	46	12	23	19	11	710
County Prosecuting Attorney, unexpired term. Augustus P. Hardy	23	17	78	179	17	33	12	17	59	37	17	57	53	46	12	23	19	11	710
County Surveyor, unexpired term. Martin Slack	22	17	77	179	17	33	12	17	59	37	17	57	53	46	12	23	19	11	710
County Treasurer, unexpired term. Martin Slack	23	17	77	179	17	33	12	17	59	37	17	57	53	46	12	23	19	11	710
One Selectman. Richard Bentley	23	17	78	179	17	33	12	17	59	37	17	57	53	46	12	23	19	11	710
Superintendent of District Schools. Moroni M. Snow	23	17	78	179	17	33	12	17	59	37	17	57	53	46	12	23	19	11	710
Jos. Orton	23	17	77	177	17	32	12	17	59	37	17	57	53	46	12	23	19	11	689
Arthur B. Cort	21			2															23

THE TERRITORY OF UTAH.   105

WASHINGTON COUNTY.

PRECINCTS.	For Justices.	No. of Votes. Full Term	No. of Votes. Unex.Term	For Constable.	No. of Votes. Full Term	No. of Votes. Unex.Term
Silver Reef	Julius Jordan	107		J. P. Cox	63	
" "				Al. Thorne	46	
Leeds	J. P. Wilkinson	17		David McMullen	17	
Washington	Jos. H. Crawford		78	Simeon A. Dunn		78
"	Levi M. Harmon		78			
St. George	Joseph Orton		120	Augustus P. Hardy	78	
" "	Moroni Snow	120				
Price	Samuel Miles	17		Archibald Sullivan	17	
Gunlock	Franklin O. Holt		12	Jeremiah Leavitt		12
Hebron	O. W. Huntsman		17	John S. Lamb		17
Pine Valley	Robert Lloyd		59	H. Y. Burgess		59
Pinto	John H. Harrison		37	Chas. E. Knell		37
New Harmony	Wm. A. Redd	17		James F. Pace	17	
Virgin City	Ianthus P. Richards		57	Jos. Workman		57
Toquerville	Lorenzo Y. Slack	52		Augustus M. Slack	51	
Rockville	David F. Stout		46	John P. Terry	46	
Duncan's Retreat	Robert W. Reeve	12		John M. Wright	12	
Grafton	Samuel Stanworth		23	Alonzo Russell		23
Springdale	Almon Draper	19		John H. Petty	19	
Shonesburg	Alfred Misner	11		Ira Beal	11	

	For Fence Viewers.		
Leeds	R. H. Ashby	12	
"	John Brown	12	

WEBER COUNTY.

COUNTY OFFICERS.	Ogden.	Lynne.	Harrisville.	Plain City.	West Weber.	North Ogden.	Hooper.	Eden.	Uintah.	Riverdale.	Huntsville.	Marriott.	Slaterville.	Wilson.	Pleasant View.	Total.
Judge of Probate, unexpired term. Lewis W. Shurtleff	895	73	106	134	92	119	157	72	22	63	140	37	92	57	75	2134
Clerk of the County Court, unexpired term. Chas. C. Richards	895	73	106	133	92	118	157	72	22	63	139	37	92	55	75	2137
One Selectman, unexpired term, one year. Brigham H. Bingham	894	73	105	133	92	119	157	72	22	63	140	37	92	57	75	2132
One Selectman, unexpired term, two years. Nathaniel Montgomery	895	73	106	133	92	119	157	72	22	63	140	37	92	57	75	2133
Assessor, unexpired term. Hyrum Belknap	895	73	106	133	92	119	157	72	22	63	140	37	92	57	75	2133
Sheriff, unexpired term. Thos. J. Stevens	890 / 5	73	103 / 3	121 / 15	92	118	157	72	22	62 / 1	140	37	63 / 29	57	75	2082 / 52
Coroner, unexpired term. Wm. Brown	896	73	106	133	92	119	157	72	22	63	140	37	92	57	75	2134
County Prosecuting Attorney, unexpired term. Mark Hall	895	73	105	132	92	116 / 2	157	72	22	63	140	37	92	57	75	2126 / 2
Franklin D. Richards	896	73	106	133	92	119	157	72	22	63	140	37	92	57	75	2133
One Selectman. Geo. Dean	892	73	106	133	92	119	157	72	22	63	139	37	92	57	75	2129
One Selectman. Robert McQuarrie	896	73	106	133	92	119	157	72	22	63	140	37	92	56	75	2133
County Surveyor, unexpired term. Washington Jenkins	897	73	106	133	92	119	157	72	22	63	140	37	92	57	75	2135
Superintendent of District Schools. Edward H. Anderson																

THE TERRITORY OF UTAH.

WEBER COUNTY.

PRECINCTS.	For Justices.	No. of Votes. Full Term	No. of Votes. Unex. Term	For Constable.	No. of Votes. Full Term	No. of Votes. Unex. Term
Ogden	Thos. D. Dee	897		Moroni F. Brown		895
Lynne	Fred'k A. Miller	72		Jas. Hanop	73	
Harrisville	Noah L. Shurtleff	104		Alfred K. Dabell	105	
"	Wm. C. Rosson	3		Lyman Keys	2	
Plain City	Wm. L. Stuart	133		Wm. Knight	133	
"	Edward Goddard	3		John Coy	3	
West Weber	Hans D. Petterson		90	Robt. McFarland		92
North Ogden	Nath'l Montgomery	119		John Godfrey	120	
Hooper	Jas. Johnson	157		Wm. J. Belknap	157	
Eden	Henry J. Fuller		72	M. E. Heninger	72	
Uintah	Byron L. Bybee	21		Hyrum F. Stoddard		22
"	Samuel Dye	2				
Riverdale	Richard Dye		63	Franklyn Watson	63	
Huntsville	Geo. Halls	140		John Grow	140	
Marriott	Thos. Saulisbury	37		Caleb Parry	35	
Slaterville	Jas. Hutchins		62	Alex. Hunter	63	
"	Wm. A. Richardson		29	Fred'k L. Hoy	29	
Wilson	Samuel Purdy		57	John E. Stoker	57	
Pleasant View	Wylie G. Cragun	75		John A. Wade	71	
"				Wilson Cragun	4	

WASATCH COUNTY.

COUNTY OFFICERS.	Heber.	Midway.	Charleston.	Wallsburgh.	Pleasant Valley.	Total.
Judge of Probate, unexpired term.						
T. H. Giles..................................	123	49	21	64		257
T. S. Watson................................	84	54	20	12		170
Clerk of the County Court, unexpired term.						
Jas. A. Shelton.............................	208	97	41	76		422
One Selectman, unexpired term, two years.						
Geo. W. Clyde..............................	208	97	41	76		422
Assessor and Collector, unexpired term.						
Thos. Hicken, Jr...........................	208	97	41	76		422
Coroner, unexpired term.						
John McDonald.............................	208	97	41	76		422
Sheriff, unexpired term.						
John Clyde..................................	124	39	21	71		255
Richard Jones..............................	84	58	20	5		167
County Prosecuting Attorney, unexpired term.						
Jos. Kirby...................................	110	42	21	69		242
Jos. R. Murdock...........................	95	55	20	7		177
County Surveyor, unexpired term.						
Wm. Buys...................................	208	97	41	76		422
One Selectman.						
A. J. Alexander............................	208	97	41	76		422
Superintendent of District Schools.						
Attewall Wootton..........................	207	97	41	76		422

PRECINCTS.	For Justices.	No. of Votes. Full Term.	Unex.Term.	For Constable.	No. of Votes. Full Term.	Unex.Term.
Heber............	T. S. Watson......	125		John H. Murdock.	207	
"	A. C. Hatch.......	208		David N. Murdock.	207	
Midway..........	Thos. Todd, Jr.....	81				
"	Moroni Gerber.....	95		S. T. Epperson...	97	
Charleston.......	E. Richman........	41		Wm. Daybell.....	41	
Wallsburgh......	D. C. Wray........	75		Heber Timothy...	74	
	For Fence Viewers.					
Midway..........	Wm. Coleman...........................				96	
"	Chas. Gurney............................				97	
Charleston......	Jas. Price.................................				41	
"	Wm. Bagley..............................				39	

A LETTER.

SALT LAKE CITY, UTAH, August 24th, 1883.

HON. H. M. TELLER, *Secretary of the Interior, Washington, D. C.:*

SIR—I have the honor to inform you that the Report upon the Registration of voters in June last, the election for Members of the Legislative Assembly, and other officers, held on the 6th day of the present month, in this Territory, and the full proceedings of this Commission in connection therewith, will, from necessity, be delayed for a time. However, we think it will be proper to say now, in advance of our regular report, that the law known as the "Edmunds Act," so far as we have been responsible for its execution, has been carefully, but rigidly enforced this year, as it was last. No person living in polygamy has been permitted to vote at any election, or to be voted for, for any office; and while only three convictions in prosecutions against polygamists under the Act of 1862, have been secured, nearly or quite fifteen thousand persons have been disfranchised on account of polygamic practices, through the operations of the law as administered by this Commission.

Ten suits for damages have been instituted against the Commission, by certain Mormons whose names were rejected at the first registration, and who were not permitted to vote at the election in November, 1882, because they refused to comply with the Rules and Regulations, prescribed under the law by the Commission, for the proof of the eligibility of all voters. It is understood that these suits have been brought for the purpose, primarily, of testing the constitutionality of this law, and secondarily, to determine the legality of our acts thereunder.

The first hearing in these cases will be had early in October.

It is deemed advisable to withhold our regular report until the court here shall have heard and passed upon these cases.

Moreover, certain phases of the general situation here have presented themselves through the recent election, and in other ways, in the present year, which will require to be carefully considered before the Commission will be prepared to make the full and comprehensive report which the President and Congress will undoubtedly desire, and the Commission will wish to make. Such a report will be prepared and forwarded, in ample time for the use of the President in communicating with Congress at the commencement of its session, in December next.

Very respectfully, your obedient servant,

ALEXANDER RAMSEY.

By order of the Commission.

ANNUAL REPORT.

WASHINGTON, D. C., October 30, 1883.

SIR: The Board of five Commissioners appointed by the President under the provisions of the act of March 22, 1882, entitled "An act to amend section 5352 of the Revised Statutes of the United States in reference to bigamy, and for other purposes," respectfully submit the following report:

Before proceeding with the account of the transactions of the Board since our last report to the Interior Department, we deem it advisable to make a brief statement of the former legislation of Congress in relation to bigamy or polygamy. There is no doubt that "plural marriage" was practiced to a considerable extent among the Mormons from the time of their first immigration to the Great Salt Lake Valley in 1847. It was in 1852 that it was first publicly proclaimed as a tenet of the church by alleged "divine revelation" by Brigham Young, president of the church, and governor of Utah Territory under the appointment of President Fillmore.

After the lapse of ten years, namely, on July 1, 1862, an act was passed by Congress which provides that "every person having a husband or wife living, who marries another, whether married or single, in a Territory or other place over which the United States have exclusive jurisdiction, is guilty of bigamy, and shall be punished by a fine of not more than $500, and by imprisonment for a term not more than five years."

Under this law there have been very few convictions, not more than three, as we are advised, for a period of over twenty years, which is due largely to the fact that a great majority of the community are in sympathy with the accused. In this connection we deem it proper to say that no reflection is intended to be cast upon the judges or other officers of justice in Utah appointed by the Government. Doubtless they have done the best they could with such means and legal measures as were furnished by the Government.

The law of March 22, 1882, is much more comprehensive. In addition to repeating the same penalty for entering into the polygamic relation, it amends the former law by providing a penalty "against any man who simultaneously, or on the same day, marries more than one woman," such cases having occurred in Utah, and the former law not providing for such "simultaneous" nuptials. Also, the present law provides a penalty for "unlawful cohabitation," which was intended to meet the case of a continuance of the polygamic relation, for it was held by the courts, under the former law, that a man living in a polygamic relation could not be convicted after the three years' statute of limitations had expired from the time of entering into the plural marriage. Besides, new sections are introduced into the present act relating to the qualification of jurors, amnesty to offenders, and the legitimation of children born before January 1, 1883.

With the execution of those provisions of the act thus far adverted to, this Commission have nothing to do; and there is a general misapprehension in the public mind as to the extent of our authority, which, though important and difficult of execution, is much more circumscribed and limited than many suppose. Our whole authority is set forth in the ninth or last section of the law, which is to be construed in connection with the preceding section, and perhaps some other sections of the act.

The eighth section provides that—

No polygamist, bigamist, or any person cohabiting with more than one woman, and no woman cohabiting with any of the persons described as aforesaid in this section, in any Territory or other place over which the United States have exclusive jurisdiction, shall be entitled to vote at any election held in any such Territory or other place, or be eligible for election or appointment to, or be entitled to hold any office or place of public trust, honor, or emolument in, under, or for any such Territory or place, or under the United States.

The ninth and last section is as follows:

SEC. 9. That all the registration and election offices of every description in the Territory of Utah are hereby declared vacant, and each and every duty relating to the registration of voters, the conduct of elections, the receiving or rejection of votes, and the canvassing and returning of the same, and the issuing of certificates or other evidence of election, in said Territory, shall, until other provisions be made by the legislative assembly of said Territory, as is hereinafter by this section provided, be performed, under the existing laws of the United States and said Territory, by proper persons, who shall be appointed to execute such offices and perform such duties by a Board of five persons, to be appointed by the President, by and with the advice and consent of the Senate, not more than three of whom shall be members of one political party, and a majority of whom shall be a quorum. The members of said Board so appointed by the President shall each receive a salary at the rate of three thousand dollars per annum, and shall continue in office until the legislative assembly of said Territory shall make provision for filling said offices as herein authorized. The Secretary of the Territory shall be the Secretary of said Board, and keep a journal of its proceedings, and attest the action of said Board under this section. The canvass and return of all the votes at elections in said Territory for members of the legislative assembly thereof shall also be returned to said Board, which shall canvass all such returns and issue certificates of election for those persons who, being eligible for such election, shall appear to have been lawfully elected, which certificates shall be the only evidence of the right of such persons to sit in such assembly: *Provided*, That said Board of five persons shall not exclude any person otherwise eligible to vote, from the polls on account of any opinion such person may entertain on the subject of bigamy or polygamy, nor shall they refuse to count any such vote on account of the opinion of the person casting it, on the subject of bigamy or polygamy, but each house of such assembly, after its organization, shall have power to decide upon the election and qualifications of its members. And at or after the first meeting of said legislative assembly, whose members shall have been elected and returned according to the provisions of this act, said legislative assembly may make such laws, comfortable to the organic act of said Territory, and not inconsistent with other laws of the United States, as it shall deem proper concerning the filling of the offices in said Territory declared vacant by this act.

It will thus be seen that the duties of this Commission appertain only to matters of registration and election and eligibility to office, while the punishment of the crime of polygamy is left, as under the former law, to the courts of justice.

Nor are we invested with legislative authority. Our powers are of a quasi-judicial and administrative character. But from the general terms of many parts of the act, we have been obliged to exercise a considerable latitude of discretion to make the act effectual, confining ourselves within the limits of the law, according to our best judgment.

We have heretofore communicated to the Department of the Interior the difficulties we encountered on entering upon our duties last year; also the measures we adopted for excluding polygamists from registration and from the polls, and that we had excluded some twelve thousand men and women from registration and voting by reason of their disqualification under this act. Pursuing the same policy, we have had equal success at the general election held on the 6th of August, 1883, in excluding polygamists from the polls.

The theory of the act of March 22, 1882, appears to be this: that a discrimination between those Mormons who practice polygamy and those who do not, placing a stigma upon the former and depriving them of the right of suffrage as well as the right to hold office, while, on the other hand, an inducement is held out to the latter class, that by abstaining from the polygamic relation they will enjoy all the political rights of American citizens, would in time have the effect of inducing great numbers of the Mormon people to refrain from plural marriage.

While such considerations are not likely to have much effect upon the elderly men who already have a plurality of wives and several families of children, they must have great weight with the young men of the Territory, many of whom are ambitious and aspiring, and would not like voluntarily to embrace political ostracism.

The leading Mormons, who are generally in polygamy, evidently perceive this tendency; and, therefore, ever since the passage of this act, they have assiduously taught their people that this measure is transient, and that it will soon be set aside by the Federal courts or by the action or non-action of Congress.

So far as we are advised, very few, if any, illegal votes have been cast in Utah since the Commission took charge of registrations and elections in August, 1882.

As to the declared objects of the act of Congress as therein set forth, so far as appertains to our duties, it is not denied that the operation of the act has been eminently successful; that is to say, the polygamists have all been excluded from the polls and from eligibility to office. Considering that during the twenty years since the anti-polygamy act of 1862 was passed, the penalties of that law have been enforced against not exceeding three persons, it would seem that in the enforcement of the present law against some twelve thousand polygamists who have been excluded from the polls, it must justly be regarded that the act has been fully and successfully executed.

Before passing from this topic, we deem it proper to observe that no person well informed in regard to Utah affairs, could reasonably have expected, at the passage of the act, that there would be an immediate change in the political situation, nor that it would have an immediate effect in destroying the practice of polygamy; but the act must necessarily have a strong influence in that direction. The very existence of the law disfranchising the polygamists must tend to destroy their influence, whenever it is understood that this is to be a permanent discrimination. Those Mormons who have the ballot will after a time be conscious of a power which they will be unwilling to use forever at the bidding of those who have it not. The fact, also, that it will be necessary to the preservation of the political influence of the "People's party" (as the Mormons style themselves) to have a large body of their members who are not polygamists, must tend in time to weaken the practice of polygamy, for every married Mormon who takes but one plural wife loses three votes for his party—his own and those of his two wives (woman suffrage being established by law in Utah). Another consideration, already adverted to, the influence upon the young men and the rising generation, is entitled to great weight. Seeing all the offices of honor, trust, and profit, such as Delegate to Congress, members of the legislative assembly, probate judges, clerks of the county courts, sheriffs, and others, many of them quite lucrative, held by monogamists, while polygamists are wholly excluded, the aspiring young men of the Territory would present an anomaly in human nature if they should fail to be strongly influenced against going into a relation which thus subjects them to political ostracism and fixes on them the stigma of moral turpitude.

The difficulty of the situation can be better understood from the fact that among the orthodox Mormons of Utah polygamy is a part of their religious faith, and while but a small per cent. of the whole adult Mormon population have actually entered into the polygamic relation, yet all the faithful believe in it as a divine revelation. The Mormons believe in the Old Testament, the New Testament, and a great deal besides, namely, the Book of Mormon, and divers so-called revelations claimed to have been received by the prophet Joseph Smith and his successors, Brigham Young and John Taylor, which are mostly printed in their Book of Doctrine and Covenants. Among these so-called revelations is one in favor of a plurality of wives.

That a doctrine and practice so odious throughout Christendom should have been upheld so many years against the laws of Congress and the sentiments of the civilized world, is one of the marvels of the nineteenth century, and can be scarcely appreciated even by those who are familiar with the world's history in relation to the difficulties of governmental control or suppression of religious fanaticism.

Certainly, no government can permit a violation of its laws under the guise of religious freedom; and while Congress may not legislate as to mere matters of *opinion*, yet it may denounce and punish as crimes those *actions* which are in violation of social duties or subversive of good order. It was upon this principle that the Supreme Court of the United States held the anti-polygamy law of 1862 to be valid and constitutional. (Reynolds vs. The United States, 8 Otto.)

The right of Congress to suppress this great evil is undoubted. It is equally plain that the dignity and the good name of this great Government among the nations of the earth demand such Congressional action as shall effectually eliminate this national disgrace.

In our report of November 17, 1882, we made several recommendations, which were substantially incorporated into Senate bill No. 2238 of the last session of Congress, reported by the Judiciary Committee, December 13, 1882. This bill, however, contains some other provisions besides those mentioned, and we hope that the proposed measure as a whole will receive the favorable consideration of Congress at its next session. The recommendations above referred to—re-submitted as a part of this report—are as follows:

In our judgment, a marriage law enacted by Congress would be an efficient auxiliary in the suppression of polygamy. It is asserted and generally believed by non-Mormons in this Territory that plural marriage is still practiced here in secret. We would recommend that Congress enact a law declaring all future marriages in this Territory null and void unless they are contracted and evidenced in the manner provided by the act. For example: that all marriages shall be solemnized in certain designated public places, and witnessed by such persons and registered in such public offices as to make the proof of marriage morally certain; providing, also, that the person officiating in the marriage ceremony, together with the parties and witnesses, shall make their affidavits against polygamy, and set forth the time and place and other particulars relating to the marriage, or allow marriages to be solemnized in private, but with the like guarantees of registration, affidavits, witnesses, etc., and in either case providing penalties for violation of the act by any of the persons concerned therein. In making this suggestion we omit the details, which can readily be supplied by reference to the marriage acts of most of the States.

In our former report we adverted to the law of this Territory conferring on women the right of suffrage. This law was enacted by the Territorial legislature some twelve years ago. Of course, it is competent for Congress to repeal or annul this law. Without expressing any opinion on the question of women suffrage in general, we are satisfied that, owing to the peculiar state of affairs in Utah, this law is an obstruction to the speedy solution of the vexed question.

In the prosecution of polygamy cases here it is difficult to prove the first or legal marriage. We would suggest as a remedy that the first or legal wife be declared by act of Congress a competent witness in such prosecutions.

Under the act of Congress by virtue of whose provisions this Commission was appointed, the people of Utah appear to be put upon probation until a legislative assembly elected under the provisions of the act shall meet and pass the requisite laws concerning registration and election.

If, however, the next session of the legislative assembly, elected under the act of Congress, shall fail to respond to the will of the nation, Congress should have no hesitation in using extraordinary measures to compel the people of this Territory to obey the laws of the land.

The present legislature, chosen at the August election, is composed wholly of Mormons, none of whom, however, *live* in polygamy. This legislature will convene in January next. It will be their duty, under the act of 1882, to adopt measures, in conformity with the provisions of that law, for the suppression of polygamy. Whether the legislature will take such action, may not properly be discussed by us in advance of the opportunity given them by the law to do so. If they shall fail in this respect when the time shall come for them to act, this Commission will be prepared to recommend, and Congress certainly will not delay the adoption of, the most stringent measures compatible with the limitations of the Constitution that may be considered necessary for the suppression of this great evil. In view of the fact that this contingency might come, we have already given the subject of such further legislation much study and reflection, and will be ready at the proper time, if the case requires, to promptly present our views for the consideration of the President and Congress.

In the interim between the November election for Delegate to Congress and the general election in August, 1883, municipal elections were held in a number of cities and towns, under rules and orders of this Board.

But the most important election was that of August 6, 1883, a general election for members of the legislative assembly, probate judges, clerks of the county courts, assessors and collectors, county recorders, sheriffs, county treasurers, county superintendents of district schools, and other county officers, and many precinct officers, numbering in all nine hundred and sixty that were elected, all of whom, as well as all the voters, are monogamists.

In June, prior to the election, the Commission caused a revision of the registration to be made in all the precincts of the Territory, excluding all polygamists from the lists, an abstract of which, marked "A," page 65, is hereto appended.

The election was conducted, in general, in a quiet and orderly manner. The total number of votes cast was 21,961, against 27,923 at the last November election. The principal falling off in the vote was on the part of Gentiles, or Liberal party. In November the total vote of the People's (or Mormon) party was 23,039; Liberal, 4,884. In August, 1883, the total vote of the People's party was 20,508; Liberal, 1,453; from which it appears that large numbers of the Liberals refrained from voting, a fact much to be regretted, for the reason that it is believed that by proper effort and "good management," one or more non-Mormons might have been elected to the legislative assembly, who would have the opportunity of putting the majority on record.

In pursuance of the ninth section of the act of Congress, the Commission appointed a board of five canvassers to canvass the returns of the election, except those for members of the legislative assembly, which under the act are to be canvassed by this Commission.

After public notice in the newspapers, the said board of canvassers assembled, with the members of this Commission, at Salt Lake City, and the election returns were canvassed, the result ascertained, and certificates of election were awarded.

Recently some ten suits were instituted in the Third District Court of Utah, by Mormons, against the members of this Commission, complaining that they had been unjustly deprived of the right to register and vote. These are understood to be test cases, designed to contest the constitutionality of the Edmunds act, as well as the legal construction which we put upon its provisions. These suits are still undecided, and are likely to be appealed to the Supreme Court of the United States.

It has been asserted that polygamic marriages have increased since the passage of the Edmunds act; on the contrary, we have the opinion of many Mormons and non-Mormons that they have comparatively decreased since the passage of said act. After diligent inquiry, we believe the latter conclusion is correct. But the Utah legislature will have the opportunity of satisfying the country on this particular subject by passing such a public marriage act as that which we have suggested to Congress.

By this and such other legislation as we have indicated, they will give the Government assurance of their loyalty and patriotism, and avert a contest that cannot but result in their discomfiture.

In concluding this report we consider it proper to commend the zeal of the Governor of Utah in his efforts to enforce the law.

ALEX. RAMSEY.
A. S. PADDOCK.
G. L. GODFREY.
A. B. CARLTON.
J. R. PETTIGREW.

Hon. H. M. Teller,
  Secretary of the Interior.

ORDER

ADOPTED JANUARY 17th, 1884.

ORDERED, That for the purpose of securing to every legal voter the privilege of voting at the election to be held on February 11th, 1884, in and for Salt Lake City, T. C. Bailey, acting as Registration Officer for said city, is hereby directed to enter upon the Registry Lists of said city, at his office, next door to the United States Land Office, No. 21 W. Second South street, from this date, and until the evening of Thursday, January 24th, 1884, the names of all legal voters whose names are not now on the Registration Lists, upon subscribing to the required oath.

It is further ordered that this Order be published in all the daily papers of this city.

ORDER

ADOPTED JANUARY 22d, 1884.

ORDERED, That the Registration Officers of this Territory shall proceed to the revision of the Registration Lists, in pursuance of the local law, and rules and regulations to be issued by this Commission.

SUPPLEMENTAL RULES

ADOPTED JANUARY 23d, 1884.

RULE I. The County Registration Officers shall forthwith procure from the Clerk of the County Court of their respective counties the last preceding Registry List on file in his office, and each by himself or deputy proceed to the revision of the same, and for this purpose visit every dwelling house each precinct and make careful inquiry if any person whose name is on his list has died, or removed from the precinct, or is otherwise disqualified as a voter of such precinct, and if so, to erase the same therefrom; or whether any qualified voter resides therein whose name is not on his list, and if so to add the same thereto, on such voter taking and subscribing the oath or affirmation heretofore prescribed by the Commission.

SUPPLEMENTAL INSTRUCTIONS

ADOPTED JANUARY 23d, 1884.

The Registration Officers and their Deputies are required :

1st. To carefully preserve the Registration List for each precinct for use at the June revision.

2d. It is expected that the work in ———————— precinct, ———————— County, will be performed wi hin ———————— days.

3d. To make diligent inquiry and report to this Commission the names of all persons, male and female, who they have good reason to believe have entered into the Polygamic relation since March 22d, 1882.

4th. The County Registration Officers and their Deputies shall receive compensation as follows : For County Registration Officers, $4 per day ; for each Deputy Registration Officer, $3 per day ; the compensation to be paid for the time during which said officers have been necessarily employed in the discharge of their duties ; and said officers are authorized to administer all oaths required in the registration.

www.ingramcontent.com/pod-product-compliance
Lightning Source LLC
Chambersburg PA
CBHW020126170426
43199CB00009B/650